SCOTLAND

CARAVAN & CAMPING

The open road... fresh air and freedom... the friendly community feel of a camping and caravan park... the instant friendships struck up by children, usually on their bikes or at the play area... lighting the barbecue, fetching the water – on a camping or caravan holiday, even the chores seem like good fun!

Scotland is a fine country for enjoyable outdoor holidays, with hundreds of parks in glorious locations, from small towns and villages to the banks of lochs and rivers, from cities to grassy dunes overlooking sandy beaches and faraway islands. Some sites are lively and busy, others remote, tiny and peaceful. Standards are high, with facilities improving every year.

A good way to sample this type of holiday is to hire a caravan holiday-home, based on a park, a croft or farm. They're spacious, well-equipped, and often positively luxurious. For all round excellence, look out for units with the Thistle Award – details on page vii.

Where to Stay...?

250 answers to the age-old question!

Revised annually, offering around 20,000 pitches – this is the most comprehensive guide to camping and caravan parks in Scotland.

For the first time, every holiday park in the guide has been graded by Scottish Tourist Board inspectors. See page vi for details of our quality assessment schemes. Individual caravan holiday homes – those situated on private land, or which are privately owned, although sited on a holiday park – are also inspected to ensure that minimum standards are met.

Accommodation is listed

• by location (in the case of isolated country properties, this is the nearest town or village)

• in alphabetical order

The maps on pages xxxv and xl show all the locations around Scotland which have entries in the guide.

Learn to use the symbols in each entry – they contain a mine of information! You can use them to check on facilities from four-poster beds to swimming pools, from babysitting services to access for disabled visitors. (There is a key on the back flap.) Naturally, it is always advisable to confirm with the establishment that a particular facility is still available.

Prices shown are per night and based on two persons, car and touring caravan or tent, or two persons and motor caravan. Some parks charge extra for awnings, and this is stated, where appropriate. Prices for caravan holiday-homes are for one week's let, unless otherwise stated. They include VAT at the appropriate rate, and service charges where applicable.

Remember, when you accept accommodation by telephone or in writing, you are entering a legally binding contract which must be fulfilled on both sides. Should you fail to take up accommodation, you may not only forfeit any deposit already paid, but may also have to compensate the establishment if the accommodation cannot be re-let.

The prices of accommodation, services and facilities are supplied to us by the operators and were, to the best of our knowledge, correct at the time of going to press. However, prices can change at any time during the lifetime of the publication, and you should check again when you book.

Bookings can be made direct to the owner, or operator, or, usually through a travel agent, or local Tourist Information Centre (more details on page xix).

Every park in this guide has been visited by Scottish Tourist Board inspectors and graded for quality under the British Graded Holiday Parks Scheme.

All aspects of the park have been assessed for quality, and particular emphasis has been placed on cleanliness.

Each entry carried a square grid, which is easily decoded to give useful information about the park. The top line – the 'ticks' – shows the park's overall quality grading. Ticks are awarded on a rising scale of excellence.

✓ : park facilities are decorated, furnished and equipped to an acceptable standard throughout

✓✓ : park facilities are maintained, decorated, furnished and equipped to a fair standard throughout

✓✓✓ : park provides comfort and service, maintained, decorated, furnished and equipped with facilities to a good standard throughout

✓✓✓✓ : park provides comfort and service, maintained, decorated, furnished and equipped with facilities to a very good standard throughout

✓✓✓✓✓ : park provides comfort and service, maintained, decorated, furnished and equipped with facilities to an excellent standard throughout

To help you locate the top graded parks – those with four or five ticks – they are indicated with an * on the maps between pages xxxv and XL.

The remaining symbols in the grid show you which types of caravans are accepted at the park, whether tents are accepted, plus the total number of pitches available (a good indication of a park's overall size).

🚐	Pitches for touring caravans
🚐	Caravan holiday-homes on the park
🚐	Caravan holiday-homes for hire
12	Total number of pitches
A	Tents welcome
🚐	Motor caravans welcome

Thistle Awards are granted to individual caravan holiday-homes, sited on parks with the highest gradings under the British Graded Holiday Parks Scheme – those with four or five ticks. Thistle Caravans are inspected by the Scottish Tourist Board every year, to ensure that their excellent standards are maintained.

Each Thistle Caravan provides a well-equipped living area, from one to three separate bedrooms, a fully fitted kitchen with full-size cooker and fridge, and a bathroom or shower with w.c.

More and more parks around Scotland have Thistle Caravans – but they are very sought after, and tend to be booked early. To make sure you have a chance of staying in a Thistle Caravan, look now for the symbol in entries throughout this guide. A list of parks with the award is on page 84.

This symbol, standing along in an entry, means that the caravan holiday-home listed has been inspected by the Scottish Tourist Board and meets our minimum standards.

For full details of the scheme contact:
The Quality Assurance Department,
Scottish Tourist Board,
23 Ravelston Terrace,
Edinburgh,
EH4 3EU
Tel: (0131) 332 2433

Où loger?

250 réponses à l'éternelle question!

Ce livre révisé chaque année et comportant plus de 250 annonces pour 1995, soit environ 20000 emplacements, est le guide le plus complet des terrains de camping et de caravaning en Ecosse.

Pour la première fois, chaque terrain dans ce guide a été noté par les inspecteurs du Scottish Tourist Board. Reportez-vous à la page vi pour plus de détails sur nos systèmes d'évaluation de la qualité. Les caravanes individuelles à louer pour les vacances - situées sur un terrain privé ou appartenant à un particulier mais situées sur un terrain - sont aussi inspectées pour assurer le respect des normes minimums.

Les modes d'hébergement sont répertoriés

- par emplacement (dans le cas des établissements ruraux isolés, c'est la ville ou le village le plus proche)

- par ordre alphabétique

Les cartes des pages xxxv à xl montrent les endroits en Ecosse qui figurent dans ce guide.

Familiarisez-vous avec les symboles dans chaque annonce. Ce sont des mines d'informations! Vous pouvez les utiliser pour vérifier quels sont les aménagements proposés, des repas du soir aux piscines, et des services de garde d'enfants à l'accès pour les visiteurs handicapés. (Vous trouverez une légende sur la dernière page de couverture.) Evidemment, il est toujours conseillé de vérifier auprès de l'organisateur qu'un aménagement particulier est toujours disponible.

Les prix s'entendent par nuit pour deux personnes, une voiture et une caravane itinérante ou une tente, ou deux personnes et une autocaravane. Certains terrains demandent un supplément de prix pour les auvents, ce qui est indiqué le cas échéant. Les prix pour les

Les réservations peuvent être effectuées directement auprès du propriétaire ou de l'organisateur, ou, en général, par l'intermédiaire d'une agence de voyages ou d'un Tourist Information Centre de la région (pour plus de détails, reportez-vous à la page xix).

Souvenez-vous qu'accepter un hébergement par téléphone ou par écrit revient à passer un contrat légal qui lie les deux parties et doit être exécuté par celles-ci. Si vous ne prenez pas l'hébergement, vous risquez non seulement de perdre les arrhes éventuellement versées, mais aussi de devoir indemniser l'établissement s'il ne peut le relouer.

caravanes à louer s'entendent à la semaine, sauf mention contraire. La TVA au taux approprié et le service (le cas échéant) sont compris.

Les prix de l'hébergement, du service et des aménagements nous ont été fournis par les organisateurs et étaient, à notre connaissance, corrects au moment d'imprimer. Cependant, les prix sont susceptibles de changer à tout moment pendant la durée de vie de la publication et il est donc bon de les revérifier au moment de réserver.

SYSTEMES D'ASSURANCE DE LA QUALITE

Chaque terrain dans ce guide a reçu la visite des inspecteurs du Scottish Tourist Board et a été noté en fonction de sa qualité dans le cadre du British Graded Holiday Parks Scheme.

Tous les aspects du terrain ont été évalués sur le plan de la qualité, et une importance particulière a été accordée à la propreté.

Chaque annonce comporte une grille facile à décoder fournissant des informations au sujet du terrain. La ligne du haut - les coches - indique le niveau de qualité globale du terrain. Les coches sont décernées par ordre croissant d'excellence.

✓ : Les aménagements du terrain présentent globalement un niveau acceptable de décoration, d'ameublement et d'équipement.

✓✓ : Les aménagements du terrain présentent globalement un niveau raisonnable d'entretien, de décoration, d'ameublement et d'équipement.

✓✓✓ : Le terrain fournit confort et service. Les aménagements présentent globalement un bon niveau d'entretien, de décoration, d'ameublement et d'équipement.

✓✓✓✓ : Le terrain fournit confort et service. Les aménagements présentent globalement un très bon niveau d'entretien, de décoration, d'ameublement et d'équipement.

✓✓✓✓✓ : Le terrain fournit confort et service. Les aménagements présentent globalement un excellent niveau d'entretien, de décoration, d'ameublement et d'équipement.

Pour vous aider à localiser les terrains les mieux notés - c'est-à-dire ceux ayant quatre ou cinq coches - ils sont indiqués par un * sur les cartes, pages xxxv à xL.

Les autres symboles sur la grille indiquent les types de caravane acceptés sur le terrain, si les tentes sont acceptées, ainsi que le nombre d'emplacements disponibles (une bonne indication de la taille globale d'un terrain).

🚐 Emplacements pour caravanes itinérantes

🚐 Caravanes à louer pour les vacances sur le terrain

🚐 Caravanes à louer

12 Nombre total d'emplacements

🛆 Tentes acceptées

🚐 Autocaravanes acceptées

Le "thistle" est décerné à titre individuel aux caravanes à louer pour les vacances, situées sur des terrains les mieux notés dans le cadre du British Graded Holiday Parks Scheme, c'est-à-dire ceux ayant quatre ou cinq coches. Les caravanes arborant le "thistle" sont inspectées par le Scottish Tourist Board chaque année, pour assurer le maintien de leur excellent niveau de qualité.

Chaque caravane arborant le "thistle" comprend un coin séjour bien équipé, une à trois chambres séparées, une cuisine entièrement équipée avec cuisinière et réfrigérateur de taille normale, ainsi qu'une salle de bains ou une douche avec W.C.

De plus en plus de terrains de camping et de caravaning en Ecosse proposent des caravanes arborant le "thistle", mais celles-ci sont très recherchées, et sont souvent réservées longtemps à l'avance. Pour être sûr de pouvoir séjourner dans une caravane arborant le "thistle", repérez maintenant le symbole dans les annonces se trouvant dans ce guide. Vous trouverez page 84 une liste de terrains proposant ces caravanes.

@ Ce symbole, isolé dans une annonce, indique que la caravane à louer en question a été inspectée par le Scottish Tourist Board et remplit nos critères minimums.

Pour recevoir tous les détails concernant ce système, contactez:
The Quality Assurance Department,
Scottish Tourist Board,
23 Ravelston Terrace,
Edinburgh,
EH4 3EU
Tél: (0131) 332 2433

ÜBER DIESES BUCH

Unterkunftsmöglichkeiten...

250 Angebote, aus denen Sie auswählen
können!

Hierbei handelt es sich um den
umfassendsten Führer zu
Campingplätzen und Caravan-Parks in
Schottland; dieser wird jedes Jahr
überarbeitet und enthält über 250
Einträge mit insgesamt ca. 20.000
Stellplätzen.

Erstmalig wurde jeder Ferienpark in
diesem Führer von Inspektoren des
Scottish Tourist Board gradiert.
Einzelheiten zu unseren Qualitäts-
sicherungsschemen auf Seite vi.
Individuelle Ferien-Caravans - d.h.
Caravans auf Privatgelände oder
Caravans, die sich zwar in einem
Ferienpark, aber in Privatbesitz
befinden - werden ebenfalls untersucht,
um eine Einhaltung der Mindest-
standards zu gewährleisten.

Die Aufführung von Unterkünften
erfolgt

- nach jeweiligem Ort (bei
  abgelegenen Unterkünften auf dem
  Land ist das die nächste Stadt oder das
  nächste Dorf)

- in alphabetischer Reihenfolge

Die Karten auf den Seiten xxxv bis xl
zeigen alle in diesem Führer
enthaltenen Orte in ganz Schottland.

Machen Sie sich mit den Symbolen
in jedem Eintrag vertraut, denn sie
enthalten eine Vielzahl von
Informationen! Sie können damit die
jeweiligen Einrichtungen überprüfen,
angefangen von Abendmahlzeiten zu
Swimmingpools, von Babysitterdiensten
bis Zugangsmöglichkeiten für
Behinderte. (Auf der Rückenklappe
finden Sie eine Zeichenerklärung.)
Es ist natürlich immer ratsam, sich
vom Veranstalter die Verfügbarkeit
einer bestimmten Einrichtung
bestätigen zu lassen.

Die Preise in diesem Führer gelten pro
Nacht und für zwei Personen, Auto und
Wohnwagen oder Zelt, bzw. zwei
Personen und Wohnmobil. Manche
Parks berechnen einen Aufpreis für

jedoch jederzeit nach Veröffentlichung ändern, und Sie sollten sich daher bei der Buchung nochmals erkundigen. Buchungen können direkt beim Eigentümer, Veranstalter oder gewöhnlich über ein Reisebüro oder ein Tourist Information Centre vor Ort vorgenommen werden (nähere Einzelheiten auf Seite xix).

Bitte beachten Sie, daß Sie bei telefonischer oder schriftlicher Unterkunftsannahme einen rechtsgültigen Vertrag eingehen, der von beiden Parteien zu erfüllen ist. Bei Nichtanspruchnahme der Unterkunft verfällt unter Umständen nicht nur eine bereits getätigte Anzahlung, sondern ist auch Schadenersatz zu leisten, falls eine anderweitige Vermietung der Unterkunft nicht möglich ist.

Vordächer, was ggf. angegeben ist. Falls nicht anders angegeben, gelten die Preise für Ferien-Caravans für eine einwöchige Vermietung. Die Preise enthalten ggf. Bedienung und Mehrwertsteuer zum jeweils geltenden Tarif.

Die Preise für Unterbringung, Leistungen und Einrichtungen werden uns von den Veranstaltern mitgeteilt und waren nach unserer Kenntnis korrekt zum Zeitpunkt der Drucklegung. Die Preise können sich

QUALITÄTSSICHERUNGSSCHEMEN

Jeder Park in diesem Führer wurde von Inspektoren des Scottish Tourist Board besucht und unter dem British Graded Holiday Parks Scheme nach Qualität gradiert.

Alle Aspekte des Parkes wurden nach der Qualität hin bewertet, wobei besonderer Nachdruck auf Sauberkeit gelegt wurde.

Jeder Eintrag trägt ein quadratisches Gitter, das leicht zu entschlüsseln ist und nützliche Informationen über den Park gibt. Die "Häckchen" in der obersten Zeile zeigen die allgemeine Qualitätsgradierung des Parkes. Je höher die Qualität ist, desto mehr "Häckchen" werden vergeben.

✓ : Die Einrichtungen des Parkes sind durchgehend nach einem angemessenen Standard dekoriert, eingerichtet und ausgestattet.

✓✓ : Die Einrichtungen des Parkes sind durchgehend nach einem mittelmäßigen Standard instand gehalten, dekoriert, eingerichtet und ausgestattet.

✓✓✓ : Der Park bietet Komfort und Service, und die Einrichtungen sind durchgehend nach einem guten Standard instand gehalten, dekoriert, eingerichtet und ausgestattet.

✓✓✓✓ : Der Park bietet Komfort und Service, und die Einrichtungen sind durchgehend nach einem sehr guten Standard instand gehalten, dekoriert, eingerichtet und ausgestattet.

✓✓✓✓✓ : Der Park bietet Komfort und Service, und die Einrichtungen sind durchgehend nach einem ausgezeichneten Standard instand gehalten, dekoriert, eingerichtet und ausgestattet.

Um Ihnen die Suche nach den Parks mit den Spitzengradierungen zu erleichtern - d.h. die Parks mit vier oder fünf Häckchen -, sind diese mit einem * auf den Karten zwischen den Seiten xxxv und xl markiert.

Die übrigen Symbole im Gitter zeigen welche Caravanarten im Park zulässig sind, ob Zelte zugelassen sind sowie die Gesamtzahl der verfügbaren Stellplätze (ein guter Hinweis auf die Gesamtgröße eines Parkes).

Stellplätze für Wohnwägen

Ferien-Caravans im Park

Ferien-Caravans zum Verleih

12 Gesamtzahl der Stellplätze

Zelte willkommen

Wohnmobile willkommen

"Thistle"-Auszeichnungen werden individuellen Ferien-Caravans verliehen, die in den Parks mit den höchsten Gradierungen unter dem British Graded Holiday Parks Scheme zu finden sind, nämlich den Ferienparks mit 4 oder 5 Häckchen. "Thistle"-Caravans werden alljährlich vom Scottish Tourist Board überprüft, um eine Aufrechterhaltung ihrer ausgezeichneten Standards zu gewährleisten.

Jeder "Thistle"-Caravan bietet einen gut ausgestatteten Wohnbereich, von 1 bis zu 3 separaten Schlafzimmern, eine Einbauküche mit großem Ofen und Kühlschrank sowie ein Bad oder eine Dusche mit W.C.

Immer mehr Parks in ganz Schottland haben "Thistle"-Caravans, diese sind jedoch sehr gefragt, und meistens schon früh ausgebucht. Um sicherzugehen, daß Sie die Möglichkeit zu einem Aufenthalt in einem "Thistle"-Caravan haben, achten Sie auf das Symbol in den Einträgen im gesamten Führer. Eine Liste der ausgezeichneten Parks befindet sich auf Seite 84.

@ Dieses Symbol bedeutet alleinstehend in einem Eintrag, daß der aufgeführte Ferien-Caravan vom Scottish Tourist Board überprüft wurde und unsere Mindestanforderungen erfüllt.

Für ausführliche Einzelheiten zu diesem Schema wenden Sie sich bitte an:
The Quality Assurance Department,
Scottish Tourist Board,
23 Ravelston Terrace,
Edinburgh,
EH4 3EU
Tel: (0131) 332 2433

SCOTLAND WELCOMES VISITORS WITH DISABILITIES

We want visitors with a disability to get around Scotland and enjoy its attractions, secure in the knowledge that comfortable, suitable accommodation is waiting at the end of the day. Obviously, you need to know in advance just what kind of access and facilities will be available in the accommodation you choose.

For more information about travel, accommodation and organisations to help you, write (or ask at a Tourist Information Centre) for the STB booklet Practical Information for Visitors with a Disability.

Useful advice and information can also be obtained from:

Disability Scotland
Information Department
Princes House
5 Shandwick Place
EDINBURGH EH2 4RG
Tel: (0131) 229 8632

Holiday Care Service
2 Old Bank Chambers
Station Road
HORLEY
Surrey RH6 9HW
Tel: (012934) 74535

You can be sure of a warm welcome where you see the Welcome Host sign displayed.

Welcome Host is one of the most exciting and far reaching customer programmes ever developed for the tourism industry. The aim of Welcome Host is to raise the standards of hospitality offered to you during your stay. You will see the Welcome Host badge being worn by a wide variety of people in Scotland (people who have taken part in STB's Welcome Host training programme and have given a personal commitment to providing quality service during your stay). In many organisations you will also see the Welcome Host certificate, displaying an organisation's commitment to the provision of this quality service.

Welcome Hosts are everywhere, from Shetland to Coldstream and from Peterhead to Stornoway and all places in between.

Scotland is famous for its warm welcome and Welcome Hosts will ensure you receive first class service throughout your stay. Look out for the Welcome sign.

From Scotland's natural larder comes a wealth of fine flavours.

The sea yields crab and lobster, mussels and oysters, haddock and herring to be eaten fresh or smoked. From the lochs and rivers come salmon and trout.

Scotch beef and lamb, venison and game are of prime quality, often adventurously combined with local vegetables or with wild fruits such as redcurrants and brambles. Raspberries and strawberries are cultivated to add their sweetness to trifles and shortcakes, and to the home-made jams that are an essential part of Scottish afternoon tea.

The Scots have a sweet tooth, and love all kinds of baking – rich, crisp shortbread, scones, fruit cakes and gingerbreads. Crumbly oatcakes make the ideal partner for Scottish cheeses, which continue to develop from their ancient farming origins into new – and very successful – styles.

And in over a hundred distilleries, barley, yeast and pure spring water come together miraculously to create malt whisky – the water of life.

Many Scottish hotels and restaurants pride themselves on the use they make of these superb natural ingredients – over 300 are members of the Taste of Scotland Scheme which encourages the highest culinary standards, use of Scottish produce, and a warm welcome to visitors. Look for the Stockpot symbol at establishments, or write to Taste of Scotland for a copy of their guide (£5.00 by post or £4.50 in shops).

Taste of Scotland Scheme
33 Melville Street
EDINBURGH
EH3 7JF
Tel: (0131) 220 1900

SCOTLANDS TOURIST AREAS

1. The Lowlands & Southern Uplands

2. The Central Highlands

3. The Northern Highlands & Inner Islands

4. The Outer Islands

THE LOWLANDS AND SOUTHERN UPLANDS

ANGUS TOURIST BOARD

ARBROATH ⊠
Market Place
Arbroath
Angus DD11 1HR
Tel: (01241) 872609
Jan-Dec

BRECHIN
St Ninians Place
Brechin
Angus
Tel: (01356) 623050
Apr-early Oct

CARNOUSTIE
The Library
High Street
Carnoustie
Tel: (01241) 852258
Apr-early Oct

FORFAR
40 East High Street
Forfar
Tel: (01307) 467876
Apr-early Oct

KIRRIEMUIR
1 Cumberland Close
Kirriemuir
Tel: (01575) 574097
Apr-early Oct

MONTROSE
Bridge Street
Montrose
Tel: (01674) 672000
Apr-early Oct

AYRSHIRE TOURIST BOARD

AYR ⊠
Burns House
16 Burns Statue Square
Ayr KA7 1UP
Tel: (01292) 288688
Jan-Dec

GIRVAN
Bridge Street
Girvan
Ayrshire
Tel: (01465) 4950
Apr-Oct

IRVINE
New Street
Irvine KA12 8DG
Tel: (01294) 313886
Jan-Dec

KILMARNOCK ⊠
62 Bank Street
Kilmarnock
Ayrshire
Tel: (01563) 39090
Jan-Dec

LARGS ⊠
Promenade
Largs
Ayrshire KA30 8BG
Tel: (01475) 673765
Jan-Dec

MAUCHLINE
National Burns
Memorial Tower
Kilmarnock Road
Mauchline
Ayrshire
Tel: (01290) 551916
Jan-Dec

MILLPORT ♿
28 Stuart Street
Millport
Isle of Cumbrae
Tel: (01475) 530753
Easter-Sept

TROON
Municipal Buildings
South Beach
Troon
Ayrshire
Tel: (01292) 317696
Easter-Sept

CITY OF DUNDEE TOURIST BOARD

DUNDEE ⊠ ♿
4 City Square
Dundee DD1 3BA
Tel: (01382) 434664
Jan-Dec

CLYDE VALLEY TOURIST BOARD

ABINGTON
Welcome Break Service
Area
Junction 13, M74
Abington
Tel: (018642) 436
Jan-Dec

BIGGAR &
155 High Street
Biggar
Lanarkshire
Tel: (01899) 21066
Easter-Oct

COATBRIDGE
The Time Capsule
Buchanan Street
Coatbridge
Tel: (01236) 431133
Apr-Oct

HAMILTON &
Road Chef Services
M74 Northbound
Hamilton
Tel: (01698) 285590
Jan-Dec

LANARK ⊠ &
Horsemarket
Ladyacre Road
Lanark ML11 7LQ
Tel: (01555) 661661
Jan-Dec

MOTHERWELL ⊠
Motherwell Library
Hamilton Road
Motherwell
Tel: (01698) 267676
Jan-Dec

STRATHAVEN &
Town Mill Arts Centre
Stonehouse Road
Strathaven
Tel: (01357) 29650
Apr-Oct

DUMFRIES AND GALLOWAY TOURIST BOARD

CASTLE DOUGLAS ⊠
Markethill
Castle Douglas
Tel: (01556) 502611
Easter-Oct

DALBEATTIE ⊠
Town Hall
Dalbeattie
Tel: (01556) 610117
Easter-early Oct

DUMFRIES ⊠
Whitesands
Dumfries
Tel: (01387) 253862
Jan-Dec

GATEHOUSE OF
FLEET ⊠
Car Park
Gatehouse of Fleet
Tel: (01557) 814212
Easter-Oct

GRETNA
Gateway to Scotland
M74 Service Area
DG16 5HQ
Tel: (01461) 338500
Jan-Dec

GRETNA GREEN ⊠ &
Old Headless Cross
Gretna Green
Tel: (01461) 337834
Easter-Oct

KIRKCUDBRIGHT ⊠ &
Harbour Square
Kirkcudbright
Tel: (01557) 330494
Easter-Oct

LANGHOLM ⊠
Kilngreen
Langholm
Tel: (013873) 80976
Easter-early Oct

MOFFAT ⊠ &
Church Gate
Moffat
Tel: (01683) 20620
Easter-Oct

NEWTON STEWART ⊠
Dashwood Square
Newton Stewart
Tel: (01671) 402431
Easter-Oct

SANQUHAR ⊠ &
Tolbooth
High Street
Sanquhar
Tel: (01659) 50185
Easter-early Oct

STRANRAER ⊠ &
1 Bridge Street
Stranraer
Tel: (01776) 702595
Easter-Oct

EAST LOTHIAN TOURIST BOARD

DUNBAR ✉ ♿
143 High Street
Dunbar
Tel: (01368) 863353
Jan-Dec

MUSSELBURGH ✉ ♿
Brunton Hall
Musselburgh
East Lothian
Tel: (0131) 665 6597
June-end Sept

NORTH BERWICK ✉ ♿
Quality Street
North Berwick
Dunbar
Tel: (01620) 892197
Jan-Dec

OLDCRAIGHALL ✉ ♿
Granada Service Area A1
Oldcraighall
Musselburgh
Tel: (0131) 653 6172
Jan-Dec

PENCRAIG ✉
A1
By East Linton
East Lothian
Tel: (01620) 860063
Apr-end Sept

EDINBURGH TOURIST BOARD

EDINBURGH AND
SCOTLAND
INFORMATION
CENTRE ♿
3 Princes Street
Edinburgh EH2 2QP
Tel: (0131) 557 1700
Jan-Dec

EDINBURGH AIRPORT ♿
Tourist Information
Desk
Main Concourse
Next to Bureau de
Change
Edinburgh Airport
Edinburgh EH12 9DN
Tel: (0131) 333 2167
Jan-Dec

FORTH VALLEY TOURIST BOARD

BO'NESS ✉
62 Union Street
Bo'ness
Tel: (01506) 826626
Easter-Sept

DUNFERMLINE ✉
13/15 Maygate
Dunfermline KY12 7NE
Tel: (01383) 720999
Easter-Sept

FALKIRK ✉
2-4 Glebe Street
Falkirk
Tel: (01324) 620244
Jan-Dec

FORTH ROAD
BRIDGE ✉
Queensferry Lodge
Hotel
St Margarets Head
North Queensferry
Tel: (01383) 417759
Jan-Dec

KINCARDINE
BRIDGE ✉
Pine 'N' Oak Lay-by
Airth
By Falkirk
Tel: (01324) 831422
Easter-Sept

LINLITHGOW ✉
Burgh Halls
The Cross
Linlithgow
Tel: (01506) 844600
Jan-Dec

GREATER GLASGOW TOURIST BOARD

GLASGOW ⊠
35 St Vincent Place
Glasgow G1 2ER
Tel: (0141) 204 4400
Jan-Dec

GOUROCK
Pierhead
Gourock
Tel: (01475) 639467
Apr-Sept

GLASGOW AIRPORT
Tourist Information Desk
Glasgow Airport
Paisley PA3 2ST
Tel: (0141) 848 4440
Jan-Dec

PAISLEY
Town Hall
Abbey Close
Paisley PA1 1JS
Tel: (0141) 889 0711
Apr-Nov

KIRKCALDY DISTRICT COUNCIL

BURNTISLAND ⊠
4 Kirkgate
Burntisland
Tel: (01592) 872667
Jan-Dec

KIRKCALDY ⊠
19 Whytescauseway
Kirkcaldy
Tel: (01592) 267775
Jan-Dec

GLENROTHES
Rothes Halls
Rothes Square
Glenrothes,
Fife KY7 5NX
Tel: (01592) 754954
Jan-Dec

LEVEN ⊠
The Beehive
Durie Street
Leven
Tel: (01333) 429464
Jan-Dec

MIDLOTHIAN TOURISM ASSOCIATION

DALKEITH
The Library
White Hart Street
Dalkeith
Midlothian
Tel: (0131) 663 2083
Jan-Dec

PENICUIK
Edinburgh Crystal
Visitor Centre
Penicuik
Midlothian
Tel: (01968) 673846
May-Oct

ST ANDREWS AND NORTH EAST FIFE TOURIST BOARD

ANSTRUTHER
Scottish Fisheries
Museum
Anstruther KY10
Tel: (01333) 311073
Easter, May-Sept

CUPAR &
Coal Road
Cupar
Fife KY15 5YQ
Tel: (01334) 652874
Jun-Sept

CRAIL
Museum & Heritage
Centre
Marketgate
Crail KY10
Tel: (01333) 450869
June-Sept

ST ANDREWS ✉
70 Market Street
St Andrews KY16 9NU
Tel: (01334) 472021
Jan-Dec

SCOTTISH BORDERS TOURIST BOARD

COLDSTREAM ✉ &
Town Hall
High Street
Coldstream TD12 4DH
Tel: (01890) 882607
Apr-Oct

HAWICK ✉
Drumlanrig's Tower
High Street
Hawick TD9 9EN
Tel: (01450) 372547
Jan-Dec

MELROSE ✉ &
Abbey House
Abbey Street
Melrose
Kelso TD6 9LG
Tel: (01896) 822555
Apr-Oct

EYEMOUTH ✉ &
Auld Kirk
Market Square
Eyemouth TD14 5HE
Tel: (018907) 50678
Apr-Oct

JEDBURGH ✉ &
Murrays Green
Jedburgh TD8 6BE
Tel: (01835) 863435
Jan-Dec

PEEBLES ✉ &
High Street, Peebles
Kelso EH45 8AG
Tel: (01721) 720138
Apr-Nov

GALASHIELS ✉ &
3 St Johns Street
Galashiels TD1 3JX
Tel: (01896) 755551
Apr-Oct

KELSO ✉ &
Town House
The Square
Kelso TD5 7HF
Tel: (01573) 223464
Apr-Oct

SELKIRK ✉ &
Halliwells House
Selkirk TD7 4BL
Tel: (01750) 20054
Apr-Oct

THE CENTRAL HIGHLANDS
AVIEMORE AND SPEY VALLEY TOURIST BOARD

AVIEMORE ✉ &
Grampian Road
Aviemore
Inverness-shire
Tel: (01479) 810363
Jan-Dec

GRANTOWN-ON-SPEY
✉ &
High Street
Grantown-on-Spey
Morayshire
Tel: (01479) 872773
Apr-Oct

RALIA ✉ &
A9, Nr Newtonmore
Inverness-shire
Tel: (01540) 673253
Apr-Oct

CARRBRIDGE ✉
Main Street
Carrbridge
Inverness-shire
Tel: (01479) 841630
May-Sept

KINGUSSIE ✉
King Street
Kingussie
Tel: (01540) 661297
May-Sept

BANFF AND BUCHAN TOURIST BOARD

ADEN
Aden Country Park
Mintlaw AB42 8FQ
Tel: (01771) 623037
Apr-Oct

FRASERBURGH
Saltoun Square
Fraserburgh AB43 5DA
Tel: (01346) 518315
Apr-Oct

TURRIFF
High Street
Turriff AB43 7DS
Tel: (01888) 63001
Apr-Oct

BANFF ⊠
Collie Lodge
Banff AB45 1AU
Tel: (01261) 812419
Apr-Oct

PETERHEAD
54 Broad Street
Peterhead AB42 6BX
Tel: (01779) 471904
Apr-Oct

BUTE AND COWAL TOURIST BOARD

DUNOON ⊠
7 Alexandra Parade
Dunoon PA23 9AB
Tel: (01369) 3785
Jan-Dec

ROTHESAY ⊠
15 Victoria Street
Rothesay
Isle of Bute PA20 0AJ
Tel: (01700) 502151
Jan-Dec

CITY OF ABERDEEN TOURIST BOARD

ABERDEEN ⊠ &
St Nicholas House
Broad Street
Aberdeen AB9 1DE
Tel: (01224) 632727
Jan-Dec

FORT WILLIAM AND LOCHABER TOURIST BOARD

BALLACHULISH
Ballachulish
Argyll
Tel: (01855) 811296
Apr-Oct

FORT WILLIAM ⊠ &
Cameron Square
Fort William
Tel: (01397) 703781
Jan-Dec

KILCHOAN
Argyll
Tel: (01972) 510222
Apr-Sept

MALLAIG ⊠ &
Mallaig
Inverness-shire
Tel: (01687) 462170
Apr-Sept

SPEAN BRIDGE
Spean Bridge
Inverness-shire
Tel: (01397) 712576
Apr-Sept

STRONTIAN
Strontian
Argyll
Tel: (01967) 402131
June-mid Sept

GORDON DISTRICT TOURIST BOARD

ALFORD &
Railway Museum
Station Yard
Alford AB3 8AD
Tel: (019755) 62052
Mid Apr-Oct

ELLON
Market Street Car Park
Ellon AB4 8JD
Tel: (01358) 720730
Late March-Oct

HUNTLY &
7A The Square
Huntly AB5 5AE
Tel: (01466) 792255
Mid Apr-Oct

INVERURIE
Town Hall
Market Place
Inverurie AB5 9SN
Tel: (01467) 620600
Mid Apr-Oct

INVERNESS, LOCH NESS AND NAIRN TOURIST BOARD

DAVIOT WOOD
A9
By Inverness
Tel: (01463) 772203
Apr-Oct

FORT AUGUSTUS
The Car Park
Fort Augustus
Tel: (01320) 366367
Apr-Oct

INVERNESS ⊠
Castle Wynd
Inverness IV2 3BJ
Tel: (01463) 234353
Jan-Dec

NAIRN
62 King Street
Nairn
Tel: (01667) 452753
Apr-Oct

ISLE OF ARRAN TOURIST BOARD

BRODICK ⊠
The Pier
Brodick
Isle of Arran
Tel: (01770)
302140/302401
Jan-Dec

LOCHRANZA
The Pier
Lochranza
Isle of Arran
Tel: (01770) 830320
May-Oct

Tourist information
service available on the
Ardrossan-Brodick ferry
Apr-Sept

KINCARDINE AND DEESIDE TOURIST BOARD

ABOYNE ✉
Ballater Road Car Park
Aboyne
Tel: (013398) 86060
Apr-Sept

BANCHORY ✉
Bridge Street
Banchory AB31 3SX
Tel: (01330) 822000
Jan-Dec

CRATHIE ✉
Car Park
Crathie
Tel: (013397) 42414
Apr-Sept

BALLATER ✉
Station Square
Ballater
Tel: (013397) 55306
Apr-End Oct

BRAEMAR ✉
The Mews
Mar Road
Braemar
Tel: (013397) 41600
Jan-Dec

STONEHAVEN ✉
66 Allardice Street
Stonehaven
Tel: (01569) 762806
Mid Apr-Oct

LOCH LOMOND, STIRLING AND TROSSACHS TOURIST BOARD

ABERFOYLE ✉ ♿
Main Street
Aberfoyle
Perthshire FK8 3TH
Tel: (018772) 352
Apr-Oct

ALVA
Scotland's Mill Trail
Visitor Centre
Glentana Mills
West Stirling Street
Alva FK12 5EN
Tel: (01259) 769696
Jan-Dec

BALLOCH ✉ ♿
Balloch Road
Balloch
Dumbartonshire G83
Tel: (01389) 753533
March-Nov

CALLANDER ✉ ♿
Rob Roy & Trossachs
Visitor Centre
Ancaster Square
Callander
Perthshire
Tel: (01877) 330342
March-Dec

DRYMEN
The Square
Drymen
Tel: (01360) 660068
Jan-Oct

DUMBARTON ✉
A82 Northbound
Milton
Dumbarton
Tel: (01389) 742306
Apr-Oct

DUNBLANE ✉ ♿
Stirling Road
Dunblane
Stirlingshire FK15
Tel: (01786) 824428
May-Sept

HELENSBURGH ✉ ♿
The Clock Tower
Helensburgh
Dumbartonshire
Tel: (01436) 672642
Apr-Oct

KILLIN ✉ ♿
Main Street
Killin
Perthshire
Tel: (015672) 820254
Apr-Oct

STIRLING ✉ ♿
Dumbarton Road
Stirling FK8 2QQ
Tel: (01786) 475019
Jan-Dec

STIRLING ✉ ♿
Royal Burgh of Stirling
Visitor Centre
Stirling
Tel: (01786) 479901
Jan-Dec

STIRLING ✉ ♿
Pirnhall Motorway
Service Area, Jct 9 (M9)
Pirnhall
by Stirling
Tel: (01786) 814111
March-Nov

TARBET -
LOCH LOMOND ✉
Main Street
Tarbet
Dumbartonshire
Tel: (013012) 260
Apr-Oct

TYNDRUM ✉ ♿
Main Street
Tyndrum
Perthshire FK20 8RY
Tel: (018384) 246
Apr-Oct

MORAY TOURIST BOARD

BUCKIE
Cluny Square
Buckie AB56 1AH
Tel: (01542) 834853
Mid May-Sept

CULLEN
20 Seafield Street
Cullen AB56 1SJ
Tel: (01542) 840757
Mid May-Sept

DUFFTOWN
Clock Tower
The Square
Dufftown AB55 4AD
Tel: (01340) 820501
Easter-Oct

ELGIN ✉
17 High Street
Elgin IV30 1EG
Tel: (01343) 542666
Jan-Dec

FORRES
Falconer Museum
Tolboth Street
Forres IV36 0DB
Tel: (01309) 672938
Easter-Oct

KEITH
Church Road
Keith AB55 3BR
Tel: (01542) 882634
Mid May-Sept

LOSSIEMOUTH
Station Park
Pitgaveny Street
Lossiemouth IV31 6NR
Tel: (01343) 814804
Mid May-Mid Sept

TOMINTOUL
The Square
Tomintoul AB37 9ET
Tel: (01807) 580285
Easter-Oct

PERTHSHIRE TOURIST BOARD

ABERFELDY ✉ &
The Square
Aberfeldy PH15 2DD
Tel: (01887) 820276
Jan-Dec

AUCHTERARDER ✉
90 High Street
Auchterarder PH3 1BJ
Tel: (01764) 663450
Jan-Dec

BLAIRGOWRIE ✉ &
26 Wellmeadow
Blairgowrie
Perthshire PH10 6AS
Tel: (01250)
872960/873701
Jan-Dec

CRIEFF ✉ &
Town Hall
High Street
Crieff PH7 3HU
Tel: (01764) 652578
Jan-Dec

DUNKELD ✉ &
The Cross
Dunkeld
Perthshire PH8 0AN
Tel: (01350) 727688
March-Oct

KINROSS ✉ &
Service Area Junction 6
M90
Kinross KY13 7BA
Tel: (01577) 863680
Jan-Dec

PERTH ✉ &
45 High Street
Perth PH1 5TJ
Tel: (01738) 638353
Jan-Dec

PERTH - Inveralmond &
Inveralmond
A9 Western City By-pass
Perth
Tel: (01738) 638481
Easter-Oct

PITLOCHRY ✉ &
22 Atholl Road
Pitlochry
Perthshire PH16 5BX
Tel: (01796)
472215/472751
Jan-Dec

WEST HIGHLANDS AND ISLANDS OF ARGYLL TOURIST BOARD

BOWMORE
The Square
Bowmore
Isle of Islay
Tel: (01496) 810254
Jan-Dec

CAMPBELTOWN ✉
Mackinnon House
The Pier
Campbeltown
Tel: (01586) 552056
Jan-Dec

CRAIGNURE
The Pierhead
Craignure
Isle of Mull
Tel: (01680) 812377
Jan-Dec

INVERARAY
Front Street
Inverary
Argyll
Tel: (01499) 302063
Jan-Dec

LOCHGILPHEAD
Lochnell Street
Lochgilphead
Argyll
Tel: (01546) 602344
April-Oct

TARBERT
Harbour Street
Tarbert
Argyll
Tel: (01880) 820429
April-Oct

OBAN ✉ &
Boswell House
Argyll Square
Oban
Tel: (01631) 63122
Jan-Dec

TOBERMORY
Main Street
Tobermory
Isle of Mull
Tel: (01688) 302182
Jan-Dec

THE NORTHERN HIGHLANDS AND INNER ISLANDS

CAITHNESS TOURIST BOARD

JOHN O'GROATS
County Road
John O'Groats
Tel: (01955) 611373
Apr-Sept

WICK ✉
Whitechapel Road
Wick
Tel: (01955) 602596
Jan-Dec

THURSO ✉
Riverside
Thurso
Tel: (01847) 62371
Apr-Oct

ISLE OF SKYE AND SOUTH WEST ROSS

BROADFORD
Car Park
Broadford
Isle of Skye
Tel: (01471) 822361
Apr-Oct

KYLE OF LOCHALSH
Car Park
Kyle of Lochalsh
Ross-shire
Tel: (01599) 534276
Apr-Oct

UIG
c/o Caledonian
MacBrayne
The Pier
Uig
Tel: (01470) 542404
Easter-Oct

GLENSHIEL
Glenshiel
Kyle of Lochalsh
Ross-shire
Tel: (01599) 511264
Apr-Sept

PORTREE ✉
Meall House
Portree
Isle of Skye IV51 9BZ
Tel: (01478) 612137
Jan-Dec

ROSS AND CROMARTY TOURIST BOARD

GAIRLOCH ✉ ♿
Auchtercairn
Gairloch
Ross-shire
Tel: (01445) 712130
Jan-Dec

NORTH KESSOCK ✉ ♿
North Kessock
Ross-shire
Tel: (01463) 731505
Jan-Dec

ULLAPOOL
Shore Street
Ullapool
Tel: (01854) 612135
Easter-Nov

LOCHCARRON ♿
Main Street
Lochcarron
Ross-shire
Tel: (01520) 722357
April-Oct

STRATHPEFFER ♿
The Square
Strathpeffer
Ross-shire
Tel: (01997) 421415
Easter-Nov

SUTHERLAND TOURIST BOARD

BETTYHILL ♿
Clachan
Bettyhill
Sutherland
Tel: (016412) 342
Apr-Sept

DURNESS ♿
Sango
Durness
Sutherland
Tel: (01971) 511259
Apr-Oct

LAIRG
Ferrycroft
Lairg
Sutherland IV27 4AZ
Tel: (01549) 402160
Easter-Oct

DORNOCH ✉
The Square
Dornoch
Sutherland IV25 3SD
Tel: (01862) 810400
Jan-Dec

HELMSDALE ♿
Coupar Park
Helmsdale
Sutherland
Tel: (01431) 821640
Apr-Sept

LOCHINVER ♿
Main Street
Sutherland
Tel: (01571) 844330
Apr-Oct

THE OUTER ISLANDS
ORKNEY TOURIST BOARD

KIRKWALL ⊠
6 Broad Street
Kirkwall
Orkney
Tel: (01856) 872856
Jan-Dec

STROMNESS
Ferry Terminal Building
Stromness
Orkney
Tel: (01856) 850716
Jan-Dec

SHETLAND ISLANDS TOURISM

LERWICK ⊠
Market Cross
Lerwick
Shetland ZE1 0LU
Tel: (01595) 693434
Jan-Dec

WESTERN ISLES TOURIST BOARD

CASTLEBAY
Main Street
Castlebay
Isle of Barra
Tel: (01871) 810336
Easter-Oct

TARBERT
Pier Road
Tarbert
Isle of Harris
Tel: (01859) 502011
Easter-Oct

LOCHMADDY
Pier Road
Lochmaddy
Isle of North Uist
Tel: (01876) 500231
Easter-Oct

STORNOWAY ⊠
4 South Beach Street
Stornoway
Isle of Lewis PA87 2DD
Tel: (01851) 703088
Jan-Dec

LOCHBOISDALE
Pier Road
Lochboisdale
Isle of South Uist
Tel: (01878) 700286
Easter-Oct

Getting around

Scotland is a small country and travel is easy. There are direct air links with UK cities, with Europe and North America. There is also an internal air network bringing the islands of the North and West within easy reach.

Scotland's rail network not only includes excellent cross-border InterCity services but also a good internal network. All major towns are linked by rail and there are also links to the western seaboard at Mallaig and Kyle of Lochalsh (for ferry connections to Skye and the Western Isles) and to Inverness, Thurso and Wick.

All the usual discount cards are valid but there are also ScotRail Rovers (multi journey tickets allowing you to save on rail fares) and the Freedom of Scotland Travelpass, a combined rail and ferry pass allowing unlimited travel on ferry services to the islands and all of the rail network.

InterCity services are available from all major centres, for example: Birmingham, Carlisle, Crewe, Manchester, Newcastle, Penzance, Peterborough, Preston, Plymouth, York and many others.

There are frequent InterCity departures from Kings Cross and Euston stations to Edinburgh and Glasgow. The journey time from Kings Cross to Edinburgh is around 4 hours and from Euston to Glasgow around 5 hours.

Coach connections include express services to Scotland from all over the UK; local bus companies in Scotland offer explorer tickets and discount cards. Postbuses (normally minibuses) take passengers on over 130 rural routes throughout Scotland.

Ferries to and around the islands are regular and reliable.

Contact the Information Department, Scottish Tourist Board, PO Box 705, Edinburgh EH4 3EU, or any Tourist Information Centre, for details of travel and transport.

Many visitors choose to see Scotland by road – distances are short and driving on the quiet roads of the Highlands is a new and different experience. In remoter areas, some roads are still single track, and passing places must be used. (It is an offence for a slow-moving vehicle to hold up another, and not give way.) When vehicles approach from different directions, the car nearest to a passing place must stop in or opposite it. Please do not use passing places to park in!

Speed limits on Scottish roads: Dual carriageways 70mph/112kph; single carriageways 60mph/96kph; built-up areas 30mph/48kph.

The driver and front-seat passenger in a car must wear seatbelts; rear seatbelts, if fitted, must be used. Small children and babies must at all times be restrained in a child seat or carrier.

Opening times

Public holidays: Christmas and New Year's Day are holidays in Scotland, taken by almost everyone. Scottish banks, and many offices, will close in 1995 on 1 and 2 January, 14 April, 1 and 29 May, 28 August, 25 and 26 December. Scottish towns also take Spring and Autumn holidays which may vary from place to place, but are usually on a Monday.

Banking hours: In general, banks open Monday to Friday, 0930 to 1600, with some closing later on a Thursday. Banks in cities, particularly in or near the main shopping centres, may be open at weekends. Cash machines in hundreds of branches allow you to withdraw cash outside banking hours, using the appropriate cards.

Pubs and restaurants: Licensing laws in Scotland generally allow bars to service alcoholic drinks between 1100 and 1430, and from 1700 to 2300, Monday to Saturday. Most are also licensed to open on Sundays; some open in the afternoon, or later at night. Hotel bars have the same hours as pubs except for Sunday, when they open 1230 to 1430, and 1830 to 2300. Residents in hotels may have drinks served at any time.

Telephone codes

Area codes for all numbers in the UK are scheduled to change during 1995, with the addition of '1' as a second digit in the code. (031), for example, becomes (0131); or (0383) becomes (01383). These numbers can be used from August 1994, and must be used after 16 April 1995. We have given all area codes in the new format.

If you are calling from abroad, first dial your own country's international access code (usually 00, but do please check). Next, dial the UK code, 44, then the area code except for the first 0, then the remainder of the number as normal.

Quarantine regulations

If you are coming to Scotland from overseas, please do not attempt to bring your pet on holiday with you. British quarantine regulations are stringently enforced, and anyone attempting to contravene them will incur severe penalties as well as the loss of the animal.

Scotland has a good choice of direct air links, both transatlantic and with Europe and also with UK cities. Scotland's main airports are listed below along with those locations within a 5 mile radius of the airports. All airports have good onward connections to the cities and towns in Scotland either by train, bus or airport taxis.

If you would like to stay near an airport, ie within 5 miles, this page will show you the locations to check in the guide. Although the centres of the cities served by each airport fall outwith a 5 mile radius, there are many properties within each city boundary located near the airport. Please check with Area Tourist Boards or Tourist Information Centres for properties and their exact distance from airports. The number beside each place-name refers to the maps on pages xxxiv to xl, eg 4B8 – Map 4, grid reference B8.

ABERDEEN AIRPORT
Dyce, Aberdeen AB2 0DU
Tel: (01224) 722331
Fax: (01224) 725724

Aberdeen airport is 7 miles (11km) north west from the centre of Aberdeen on the A96.

GLASGOW AIRPORT
Paisley PA3 2ST
Tel: (0141) 887 1111
Fax: (0141) 848 4586

Glasgow Airport is 8 miles (13km) from the city centre.

EDINBURGH AIRPORT
Edinburgh EH12 9DN
Tel: (0131) 333 1000
Fax: (0131) 335 3181

The airport is approximately 7 miles (11km) from the city centre.

INVERNESS AIRPORT
Highlands & Islands Airports Limited
Dalcross, Inverness IV1 2JB
Tel: (01463) 232471
Fax: (01667) 462840

The airport is 8 miles (13km) from Inverness.
4C8 Nairn
4C8 by Nairn
4C8 by Croy

PASSPORT TO THE ISLANDS

PASSPORT TO THE ISLANDS

Staying on an island is a very special experience – the ferry crossing, even if it's only a few minutes long, adds a special magic to any trip.

To find accommodation in island locations in this guide, you need to look under the name of the island itself (if it is one of the smaller ones), or under the name of the appropriate town on the island (if it is larger). On Arran, for example, locations to check include Brodick, Lamlash, Whiting Bay and so on. This index tells you the names to look up for the island that interests you, together with references for the maps on pages xxxv to xl. Happy hunting!

MAPS

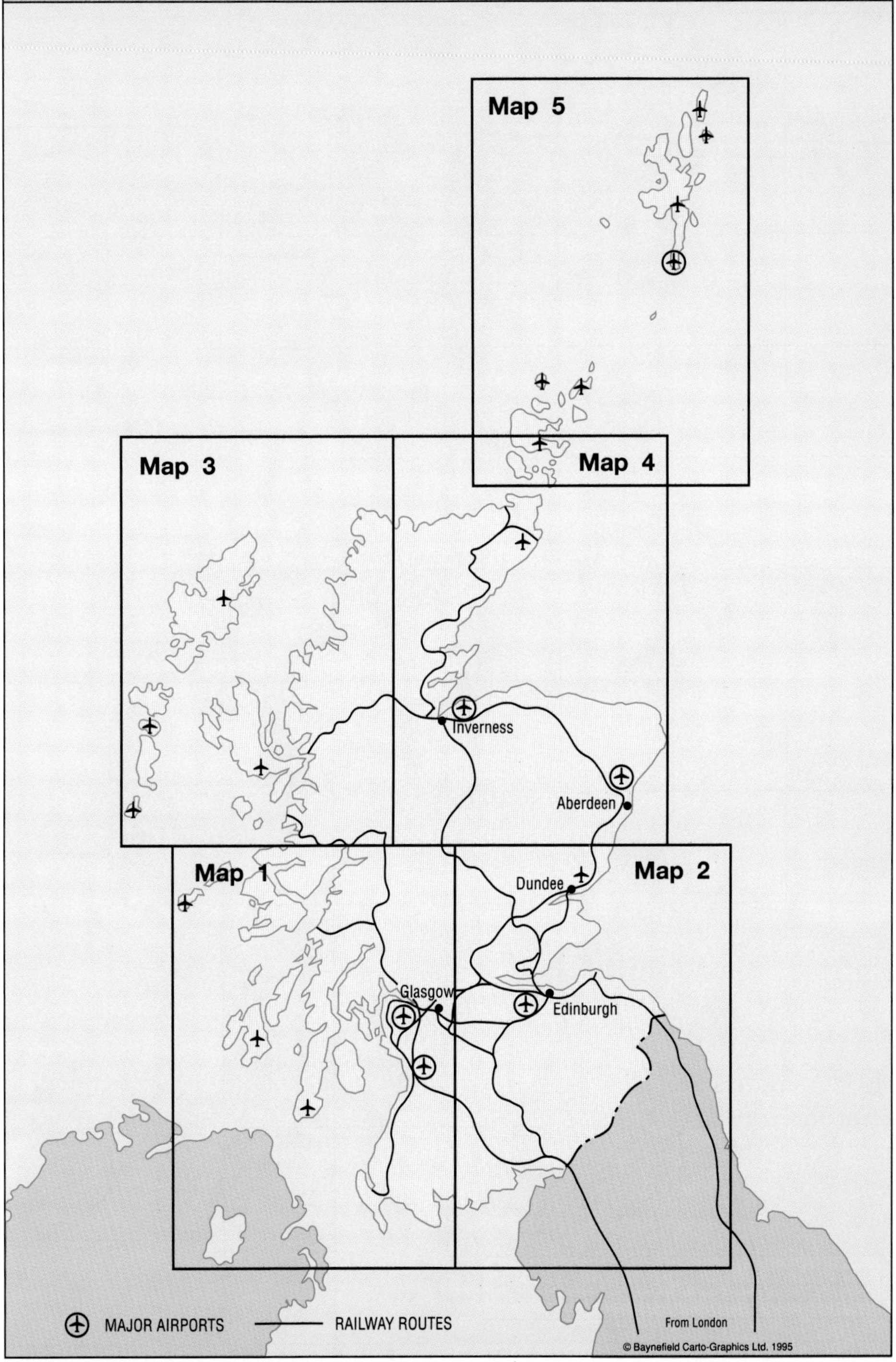

Map 5

Map 3

Map 4

Inverness

Aberdeen

Map 1

Dundee

Map 2

Glasgow

Edinburgh

⊕ MAJOR AIRPORTS ——— RAILWAY ROUTES

From London

© Baynefield Carto-Graphics Ltd. 1995

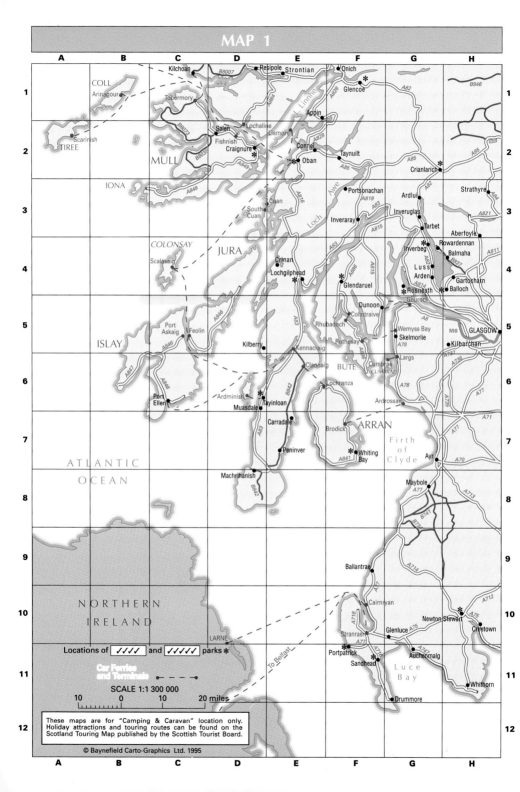

MAP 2

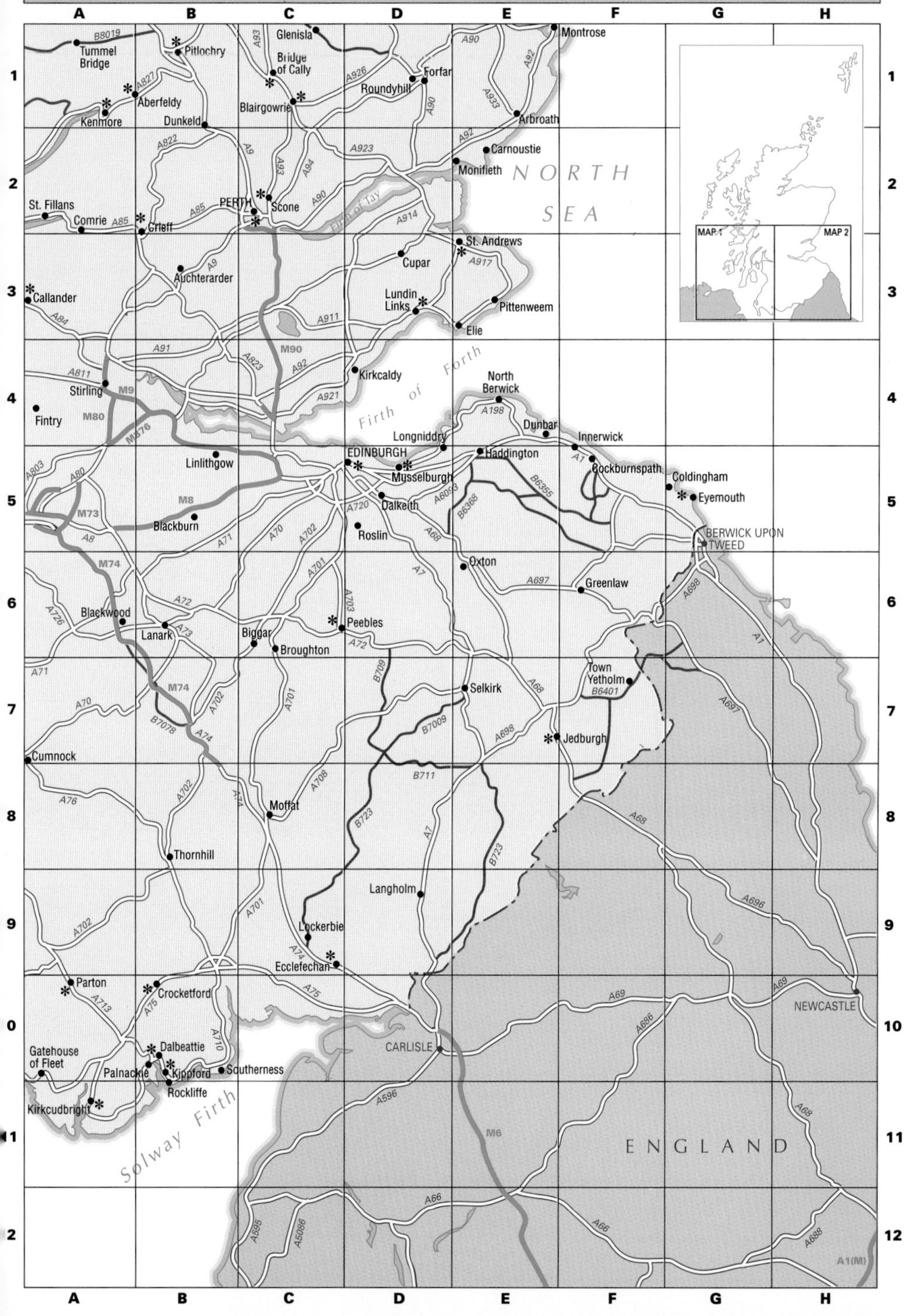

A
B
C
D
E
F
G
H
1
2
3
4
5
6
7
8
9
10
11
12
Tummel Bridge
B8019
Pitlochry
Glenisla
Bridge of Cally
Montrose
Forfar
Roundyhill
Aberfeldy
Kenmore
Blairgowrie
Dunkeld
Arbroath
Carnoustie
Monifieth
NORTH SEA
St. Fillans
Comrie
Crieff
PERTH
Scone
Firth of Tay
St. Andrews
Cupar
Auchterarder
Callander
Lundin Links
Pittenweem
Elie
Kirkcaldy
Firth of Forth
Stirling
Fintry
North Berwick
Dunbar
Innerwick
Longniddry
Linlithgow
EDINBURGH
Musselburgh
Haddington
Cockburnspath
Coldingham
Eyemouth
Dalkeith
Blackburn
Roslin
BERWICK UPON TWEED
Oxton
Greenlaw
Blackwood
Lanark
Biggar
Broughton
Peebles
Town Yetholm
Selkirk
Jedburgh
Cumnock
Moffat
Thornhill
Langholm
Lockerbie
Ecclefechan
Parton
Crocketford
Gatehouse of Fleet
Dalbeattie
Palnackie
Kippford
Southerness
Rockliffe
Kirkcudbright
Solway Firth
CARLISLE
NEWCASTLE
ENGLAND
M9
M80
M876
M90
M8
M73
M74
M6
A1(M)
A1
A7
A68
A66
A69
A74
A75
A76
A696
A697
A698
A701
A702
A703
A708
A710
A713
MAP 1
MAP 2

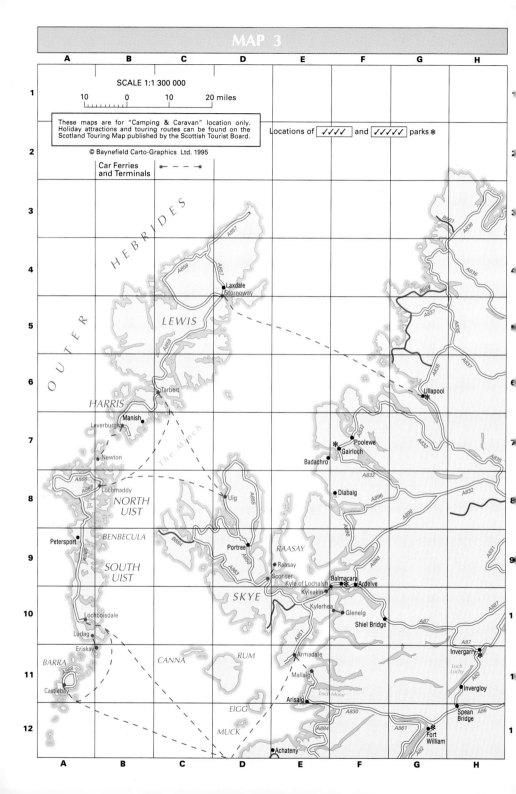

MAP 3

SCALE 1:1 300 000

10   0   10   20 miles

These maps are for "Camping & Caravan" location only.
Holiday attractions and touring routes can be found on the
Scotland Touring Map published by the Scottish Tourist Board.

Locations of √√√√ and √√√√√ parks ∗

© Baynefield Carto-Graphics Ltd. 1995

Car Ferries
and Terminals

HEBRIDES

OUTER

LEWIS

Laxdale
Stornoway

A857
A858
A867
A859

HARRIS

Tarbert

Manish
Leverburgh

Newton

The Minch

Ullapool ∗

A832

Poolewe ∗
Gairloch

Badachro

Lochmaddy

A865
A867

*NORTH
UIST*

Uig

Diabaig

A896

A832

A835
A837

B801
A838

A838

A869

A837

A835

A835

BENBECULA

Petersport

B884

Portree

RAASAY

Raasay

*SOUTH
UIST*

A865

Sconser

Kyle of Lochalsh
Kyleakin

Balmacara ∗
Ardelve

A890

A831

Lochboisdale

Kylerhea

Glenelg
Shiel Bridge

A87

Invergarry ∗

A87

*Loch
Lochy*

A82

Ludag
Eriskay

BARRA
A888

Castlebay

CANNA

RUM

Armadale

Mallaig

Loch Morar

Arisaig

Invergloy

A886

EIGG

A830

A884

A861

Spean
Bridge

A86

MUCK

Fort
William ∗

A82

Achateny

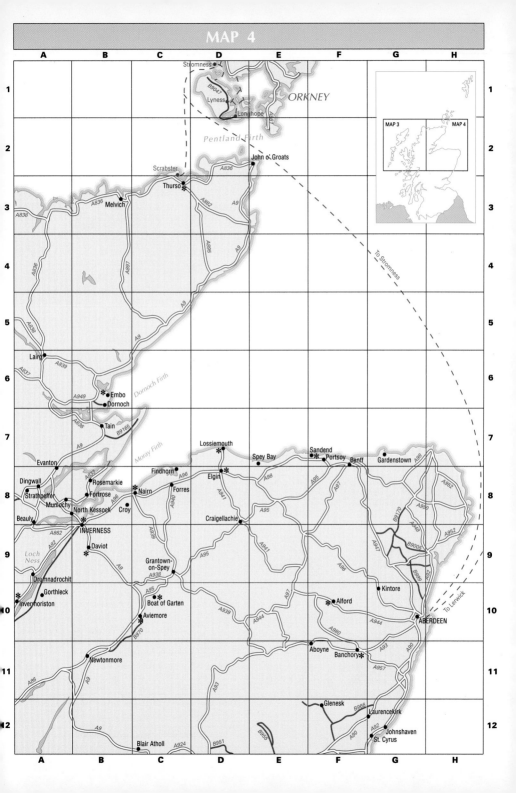

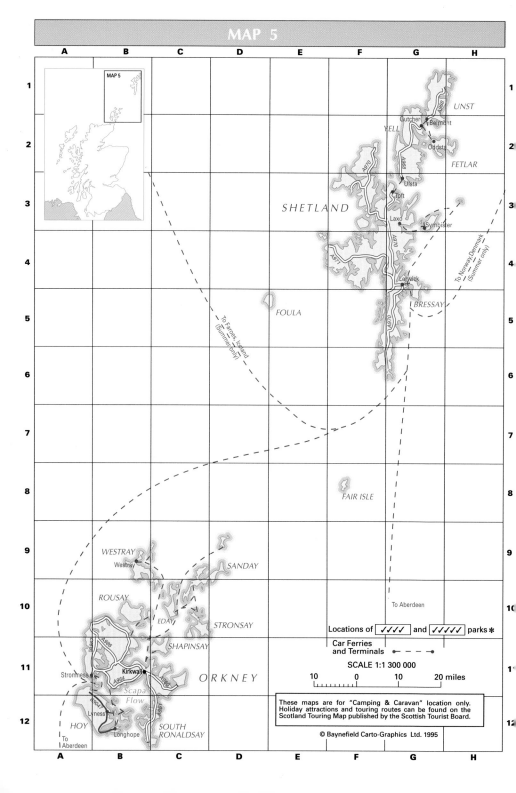

MAP 5

MAP 5

UNST
Gutcher — Belmont
YELL
Oddsta
FETLAR
Ulsta
Toft
SHETLAND
Laxo
Symbister
A970
A971
Lerwick
To Norway/Denmark
(Summer only)
BRESSAY
To Faroes, Iceland
(Summer only)
FOULA

FAIR ISLE

WESTRAY
Westray
SANDAY
ROUSAY
EDAY
STRONSAY
To Aberdeen
SHAPINSAY

Locations of ✓✓✓✓ and ✓✓✓✓✓ parks ✱
Car Ferries
and Terminals ●— — —●
SCALE 1:1 300 000
10   0   10   20 miles

Stromness
Kirkwall
A964
A960
ORKNEY
Scapa
Flow
HOY
Lyness
Longhope
SOUTH
RONALDSAY
To
Aberdeen

These maps are for "Camping & Caravan" location only.
Holiday attractions and touring routes can be found on the
Scotland Touring Map published by the Scottish Tourist Board.

© Baynefield Carto-Graphics Ltd. 1995

SCOTLAND

CAMPING & CARAVANING
1995

ABERDEEN, Map Ref. 4G10

Craighill Park, Stonehaven Road, Aberdeen, AB1 4LQ
☎ *(Aberdeen) 01224 873529 Fax: 01224 869673*
Booking Enquiries: Marywell Park, Stonehaven Road, Aberdeen
☎ *(Aberdeen) 01224 869673 Fax: 01224 869673*
5 acres, mixed, Apr-Oct, latest time of arrival 2200. Extra charge for electricity, awnings, showers.

⚓ ⚡ ⊙ ⓖ ⓘ E ⓦ Ⓟ ⚑ ☮ ✕ 🐕 ⚷ ⦿ ☂

18 tourers £6.00-8.00 or 2 motors £6.00-8.00 or 5 tents £5.00-8.00.
Total Touring Pitches 20.
2 Holiday Caravans to let, sleep 6 £180.00-200.00, total sleeping capacity 12.

Ⓜ ⚓ ⚡ 🚐 ⃞ E ⓦ Ⓟ ⚑ ☮ ✕ 🐕 ⛁ ⦰ 🝙 ⚶

1 ml S of Bridge of Dee on A90 Stonehaven road.

Hazlehead Caravan Park, Groats Road, Aberdeen, AB1 8BE
☎ *(Aberdeen) 01224 321268 (Apr-Sep)*
Booking Enquiries: Aberdeen Leisure, Beach Leisure Centre, Beach Promenade, Aberdeen, AB2 1NR
☎ *(Aberdeen) 01224 647647 (Oct-Mar) Fax: 01224 648693*
6 acres, grassy, level, sheltered, Apr-Sep, prior booking in peak periods, latest time of arrival 2200.

⚓ ⚡ ⊙ ⓖ 🚐 ⓘ ⓦ Ⓟ ⚑ ✕ 🐕 ⚶ 🝙 ⚙ ⚷ ☂

165 tourers £6.85 or 165 motors £6.85 or 165 tents £3.45-6.85.
Total Touring Pitches 165.
From Aberdeen take A944 W for 3 mls along Queen's Road.
Turn left onto Groats Road.

ABERFELDY, Perthshire, Map Ref. 2B1

Aberfeldy Caravan Park, Dunkeld Road, Aberfeldy, Perthshire, PH15 2AQ
☎ *(Aberfeldy) 01887 820662/01738 39911/639911 Fax: 01738 35225/635225*
3 acres, grassy, level, Apr-Oct, prior booking in peak periods, latest time of arrival 2000, overnight holding area. Extra charge for electricity, awnings.

⚓ ⚡ ⊙ ⓖ 🚐 ⓘ E ⓦ Ⓟ ⚑ ✕ 🐕 ⚶ ⚷ ⦿ ☂ Ⓓ

102 tourers £7.00-8.20 or 102 motors £7.00-8.20 or 50 tents £6.40.
Total Touring Pitches 102.
Leisure facilities: ✿
From Perth take A9 N for 21 mls, left at Ballinluig on to A827.
Site is on A827 at eastern approach to Aberfeldy.

Booking Enquiries: Mrs May Scott, Donafuil Farm, Keltneyburn, Aberfeldy, Perthshire, PH15 2AQ
☎ *(Kenmore) 01887 830371*
6 Holiday Caravans to let, sleep 6-8 £70.00-170.00, total sleeping capacity 26, min. let 2 nights (low season), Apr-Oct.

⚓ ⚡ 🚐 E ⓦ Ⓟ ⚑ ☮ ✕ 🐕 🏛 ⦰ 🝙 ⚶ 🎣

Leisure facilities: ► ⚑ ∪ ⚠ ⚘ ⚓
From Aberfeldy take Kinloch Rannoch road B846 for 4 mls. Farm road on right 100 yds before telephone kiosk at Coshieville.

ABERFOYLE, Perthshire, Map Ref. 1H3

100

Cobleland Campsite, Forest Enterprise, Aberfoyle, Perthshire, FK8
☎ *(Aberfoyle) 01877 382392/382383*
Booking Enquiries: Forest Enterprise, Aberfoyle, Perthshire, FK8
☎ *(Aberfoyle) 01877 382383 Fax: 01877 382694*
5 acres, grassy, stony, Apr-Oct, prior booking in peak periods, latest time of arrival 2200, overnight holding area. Extra charge for electricity, awnings, showers.

100 tourers £5.25-6.50 or 100 motors £5.25-6.50 or 100 tents £5.25-6.50.
Total Touring Pitches 100.

Leisure facilities:
Off A81 2 mls S of Aberfoyle turn off on to unclassified road. Site lies off main road adjacent to hump backed bridge.

45

Trossachs Holiday Park, Aberfoyle, Perthshire, FK8 3SA
☎ *(Aberfoyle) 01877 382614 Fax: 01877 382732*
10 acres, mixed, Apr-Oct, prior booking in peak periods, latest time of arrival 2100, overnight holding area. Extra charge for electricity, awnings.

45 tourers £6.50-9.00 or 45 motors £6.50-9.00 or 20 tents £6.50-9.00.
Total Touring Pitches 45.
12 Holiday Caravans to let, sleep 2-6 £99.00-399.00, total sleeping capacity 55, min. let 3 nights.

Leisure facilities:
3 mls S of Aberfoyle on A81 from Glasgow.

BY ABOYNE, Kincardineshire, Map Ref. 4F11

INSPECTED

Booking Enquiries: Mrs A D M Farquharson, Finzean House, Finzean, by Banchory, Kincardineshire, AB31 5ED
☎ *(Feughside) 01330 850229*
Holiday Caravan to let, sleeps 2-6 £105.75-129.25, Apr-Oct.

Take B976 from Aboyne, B974/976 from Banchory. At Finzean Stores follow unclassified road signposted Forest of Birse for 1 ml. Turn right into farm road before modern bungalow to Percie Farm.

ACHATENY, Argyll, Map Ref. 3E12

INSPECTED

Booking Enquiries: Mrs B Cameron, Branault, Achateny, Acharacle, Argyll, PH36 4LG
☎ *(Kilchoan) 01972510 284*
3 Holiday Caravans to let, sleep 4-6 £90.00-140.00, total sleeping capacity 16, min. let long weekend, Apr-Oct.

North coast of Ardnamurchan Peninsula. Turn right off B8007, 3 mls before Kilchoan, onto Kilmory Road for 2 mls.

VAT is shown at 17.5%: changes in this rate may affect prices.

ALFORD, Aberdeenshire, Map Ref. 4F10

Haughton Caravan Park, Montgarrie Road, Alford, Aberdeenshire, AB33 8NA
☎ *(Alford) 019755 62107*
18 acres, mixed, Apr-Sep, latest time of arrival 2100. Extra charge for electricity, awnings.

🕎 ๓ ⊙ ◙ ∥ ▣ 🐛 ♥ E ᵂᶜ Ⓟ ⛳ ひ ✕ ⋔ ⚠ ◊ ☻ ☗

73 tourers £6.50 or 73 motors £6.50 or 62 tents £6.50. Total Touring Pitches 135.
2 Holiday Caravans to let, sleep 6 £175.00-190.00, total sleeping capacity 12, min. let weekend.

🕎 ๓ ➡ ▢ E ᵂᶜ Ⓟ ⛳ ひ ✕ ⚠ ▯ ∅ ▤ ☒ † Ⓓ

Leisure facilities: 🔴 ⊕ ◢
Take A944 from Aberdeen. Turn right at Spar shop in Alford.

APPIN, Argyll, Map Ref. 1E1

APPIN LOCHSIDE CARAVAN PARK
Appin, Argyll PA38 4BQ   Tel: (01631) 73287 or (01631) 730287
Thistle award holiday residential caravans on lochside farm amid natural beauty. Truly magnificent situation.
10' and 12' wide models. Lodges and cottages also available. Free fishing. Boats available. Pony-trekking and hotel nearby. Ideal touring centre mid OBAN-FORT WIILLIAM. £135-£275 weekly.
Discounts to couples. Free colour brochure. (SAE Please).

Appin Holiday Caravans, Appin, Argyll, PA38 4BQ
☎ *(Appin) 01631 73287/01631 730287*
Apr-Oct.

⊙ ◙ ∥ ▣ ➡ ▥ ⚠

8 Holiday Caravans to let, sleep 2-6 from £135.00, total sleeping capacity 48, min. let weekend (low season), Apr-Oct.

🕎 ๓ ▣ ▢ E Ⓟ ⛳ ✕ ➡ ▥ ⚠ ∅ ▤ ☒

Leisure facilities: 🔴 ⊕ ▶ ◢ ◢ ∪ ◈ ⚘
15 mls N of Connel Bridge. 15 mls S of Ballachulish Bridge.

ARBROATH, Angus, Map Ref. 2E1

Red Lion Caravan Park, Dundee Road, Arbroath, Angus, DD11 2PT
☎ *(Arbroath) 01241 872038 Fax: 01241 430324*
18 acres, grassy, sandy, Apr-1 Oct, latest time of arrival 2100. Extra charge for electricity, awnings, showers.

🕎 ๓ ⊙ ◙ ▣ ▣ E ᵂᶜ Ⓟ ひ ✕ ⋔ ⚠ ❗ Ⓡ ☒ 🪣 ◊ ♫ ☻

50 tourers £7.50 or 50 motors £7.50. Total Touring Pitches 50. No tents.
Leisure facilities: 🔴 ⊕ ▶ ◢
From Dundee take A92 to Arbroath. Site on left just before town centre.

ARDELVE, Ross-shire, Map Ref. 3F9

Booking Enquiries: Mrs Catherine A MacDonald, 6 Falcon Avenue, Inverness, IV2 3TF
☎ *(Inverness) 01463 236035*
Holiday Caravan to let, sleeps 6 £75.00-110.00, Apr-Oct.

🕎 ๓ ⊙ ▢ E ᵂᶜ Ⓟ ⛳ ✕ ⋔ ∅ ▤ ☒

ARDEN, Dunbartonshire, Map Ref. 1G4

INSPECTED

Booking Enquiries: Mrs MacLeod, 12 Murray Place, Luss, Dunbartonshire, G83 8PG
☎ *(Luss) 01436860 288*
Holiday Caravan to let, sleeps 6 £130.00-150.00, Apr-Oct.

Ⓐ ℝ ☉ 🖵 E 🆆 🅿 ✕ 🅇 🖂 ⊘ 🛢 ⚒

Take A82 from Balloch N for 4 mls. Turn left onto B832 for ½ ml.
Caravan on left at Muirland Cottage.

ARDLUI, Dunbartonshire, Map Ref. 1G3

Ardlui Hotel and Caravan Park

**ARDLUI, LOCH LOMOND
DUNBARTONSHIRE
Telephone: 013014 243**

Nestling in the midst of magnificent scenery at the head of Loch Lomond, the Ardlui Caravan Park stands on the shore commanding a superb panoramic view of this most famous of Scottish Lochs. Our fleet of luxury holiday caravans are 6 or 8 berth, well equipped and connected to mains services with W.C., Shower, Fridge and Colour TV.

Hotel on site is fully licensed with two lounge bars serving meals and restaurant open to non-residents.

Laundry, children's play area, sheltered marina, boat hire, slipway, moorings, shop and petrol station.

Ardlui is an ideal centre for touring, water ski-ing, fishing, hill-walking and mountaineering.

**Brochure on request to:
Ardlui Hotel and Caravan Park, Loch Lomond,
Dunbartonshire. Tel: (0130 14) 243.**

Ardlui Caravan Park, Ardlui, Dunbartonshire, G83 7EB
☎ *(Inveruglas) 013014 243 Fax: 013014 268*
5 acres, mixed, mid Mar-Oct, latest time of arrival 2000, overnight holding area.
Extra charge for electricity, awnings, showers.

Ⓐ ℝ ➔ ☉ 🗑 ⁄ 🕮 🖵 🆆 🅿 🕁 ✕ 🅇 🏢 ⚠ 🍴 Ⓡ 🛎 ♨ ⚓ 🦢 🍴 ❤ 🕯 Ⓣ SP

10 tourers £7.00 or 10 motors £7.00 or 10 tents £5.00. Total Touring Pitches 20.
5 Holiday Caravans to let, sleep 6-8 £200.00-295.00, total sleeping capacity 32,
min. let 2 nights.

Ⓐ ℝ ➔ 🜂 🖵 E 🆆 🅿 🕁 ✕ 🅇 🏢 ⚠ 🖂 ⊘ 🛢 ⚒ 🕯 ❤ Ⓣ

Leisure facilities: ✪ 🜋 ⚓ ⤼ ⚓ ⚕
Situated on A82 at Ardlui.

ARISAIG, Inverness-shire, Map Ref. 3E11

Gorten Sands Caravan Site, Gorten Farm, Arisaig, Inverness-shire, PH39 4NS
☎ *(Arisaig) 016875 283*
6 acres, grassy, level, Apr-Sep, latest time of arrival 2300. Extra charge for electricity, awnings, showers.

Ⓐ ℝ ☉ 🗑 ⁄ 🜂 E 🆆 🅿 🛎 🕁 ✕ 🅇 🜍 🦢 🍴 ❤

40 tourers £7.50-9.00 or 40 motors £6.00-9.00 or 40 tents £6.00-8.00.
Total Touring Pitches 40.
3 Holiday Caravans to let, sleep 6 £145.00-275.00, total sleeping capacity 18,
min. let weekend (3 days).

Ⓜ Ⓐ ℝ ☉ 🖵 E 🆆 🅿 🛎 🕁 ✕ 🅇 ⊘ 🛢 ⚒ ❤ 🚲

Leisure facilities: ▶
From Fort William take A830 W for 38 mls. Turn left at signpost Back of Keppoch
and continue for ¾ ml to road end, across cattle grid.

Key to symbols
is on back flap

ARISAIG, Inverness-shire, Map Ref. 3E11

Kinloid Caravan Site, Arisaig, Inverness-shire, PH39 4NS
☎ *(Arisaig) 01687 450366*
Grassy, hard-standing, sloping, Apr-Oct. Extra charge for electricity, awnings, showers.

🔥 🛉 ➡ ☉ 🗑 ∥ 🚗 🍴 wc P ⚡ ⊙ ✕ 🐕 🦮 🔥 T SP

5 acres, 2 tourers from £4.00 or 2 motors from £4.00 or 11 tents from £4.00.
Total Touring Pitches 11.
6 Holiday Caravans to let, sleep 6 from £140.00, total sleeping capacity 36.

🔥 🛉 ➡ 🚗 ❑ E wc P ⚡ ⊙ 🐕 🏠 ⌀ 🗑 🔥 T 🧺

¹/₂ ml past Arisaig village.

AUCHENMALG, Wigtownshire, Map Ref. 1G11

Cock Inn Caravan Park, Auchenmalg, Wigtownshire, DG8 0JT
☎ *(Auchenmalg) 01581 500227*
7 acres, mixed, Mar-Oct, prior booking in peak periods, latest time of arrival 2300, overnight holding area. Extra charge for electricity, awnings.

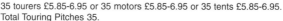

35 tourers £5.85-6.95 or 35 motors £5.85-6.95 or 35 tents £5.85-6.95.
Total Touring Pitches 35.
5 Holiday Caravans to let, sleep 6 £120.00-220.00, total sleeping capacity 30, min. let 2 nights.

Leisure facilities: 🏄 ⚓ ▶ 🎣 🚣 ∪ ✓ ☒
Park is on A747 Glenluce-Port William road, 5 mls from A75 Newton Stewart-Stranraer road.

AUCHTERARDER, Perthshire, Map Ref. 2B3

Auchterarder Caravan Park, Auchterarder, Perthshire, PH3 1ET
☎ *(Auchterarder) 01764 663119*
Booking Enquiries: Mrs S Robertson, Nether Coul, Auchterarder, Perthshire, PH3 1ET
☎ *(Auchterarder) 01764 663119*
6 acres, mixed, Jan-Dec, prior booking in peak periods, latest time of arrival 2100, overnight holding area. Extra charge for electricity, awnings.

🔥 🛉 ☉ 🗑 ∥ 🚗 🍴 E wc P ⚡ ⊙ ✕ 🐕 🏠 🐟 🔥 🍴 🥄 T D

25 tourers £6.50-7.50 or 25 motors £6.00-7.00 or 20 tents £5.00-6.00.
Total Touring Pitches 25.
Leisure facilities: 🏌 ▶ 🎣 ∪ ✓ ⛰ ✈ ⚓ ⚓ ⛷ ⛸
Join A824 from A9 (Auchterarder signpost), turn S onto B8062 (Dunning signpost) ³/₄ ml E of Auchterarder. Site 20 yds on left.

AVIEMORE, Inverness-shire, Map Ref. 4C10

Campgrounds of Scotland, Coylumbridge, Aviemore, Inverness-shire
☎ *(Aviemore) 01479 810120 Fax: 01479 810120*
9 acres, mixed, Jan-Dec, prior booking in peak periods, latest time of arrival 2300.
Extra charge for electricity, awnings.

🔥 🛉 ☉ 🗑 ∥ 🚗 🍴 E wc P ⚡ ⊙ ✕ 🐕 🐟 🔥 🍴 ⛸

17 tourers from £5.50 or 17 motors from £5.50 or 22 tents from £4.50.
Total Touring Pitches 39.
15 Holiday Caravans to let, sleep 6 from £170.00, total sleeping capacity 90.

🔥 🛉 ☉ ❑ E wc P ⚡ ⊙ ✕ 🐕 🏠 ⌀ 🗑 🔥 ⛸

AVIEMORE, Inverness-shire, Map Ref. 4C10

DALRADDY HOLIDAY PARK
By Aviemore, Inverness-shire PH22 1QB
Tel: (01479) 810330 Fax: (01540) 651380

2¹/₂ miles south of Aviemore. 25 acres of parkland with secluded pitches amongst birch woodland. Chalets or static caravans for sale or rent. Tourers and tents welcome. Licensed shop, launderette, toilet block, children's play area, facilities for the disabled.

Additional activities available nearby include golf, skiing, fishing, clay pigeon shooting, watersports, gliding, walking plus many more.

20 units, sleeps 4-6
Prices from £95 per week.

Dalraddy Holiday Park, Aviemore, Inverness-shire, PH22 1QB
☎ *(Aviemore) 01479 810330 Fax: 01540 651380*
25 acres, mixed, Dec-Oct, prior booking in peak periods, latest time of arrival 1900.
Extra charge for electricity, showers.

28 tourers £5.95-7.50 or 28 motors £5.95-7.50 or 50 tents £3.50-4.50.
Total Touring Pitches 28.
22 Holiday Caravans to let, sleep 4-6 £95.00-220.00, total sleeping capacity 86, min. let 2 nights.

Leisure facilities: ♦ ∪ ✓ ☒
3¹/₂ mls S of Aviemore on B9152 (old A9).

Glenmore Camping & Caravan Park, Forestry Commission, Glenmore, Aviemore, Inverness-shire, PH22 1QU
☎ *(Cairngorm) 01479 861271*
17 acres, mixed, mid Dec-early Nov, prior booking in peak periods, latest time of arrival 2000, overnight holding area. Extra charge for electricity.

220 tourers £5.90-7.10 or 110 motors £5.90-7.10 or 110 tents £5.90-7.10.
Total Touring Pitches 220.
Leisure facilities: ♦ ☒ ⬦ ⅄ ⬥ ⚓
Take A9 to Aviemore and turn onto B9152 S of Aviemore, then B970 to Coylumbridge. Continue on road signposted Cairngorm for 5 mls. Site on right at E end of Loch Morlich.

Speyside Highland Leisure Park
Booking Enquiries: Mrs Bruce, 2 Dell Mhor, Aviemore, Inverness-shire, PH22 1PU
☎ *(Aviemore) 01479 810230*
2 Holiday Caravans to let, sleep 6 £125.00-190.00, total sleeping capacity 12, min. let weekend, Jan-Dec.

Leisure facilities: ☃
Turn off old A9 and take B970 for 200 yds.

Key to symbols is on back flap

VAT is shown at 17.5%: changes in this rate may affect prices.

AYR, Map Ref. 1G7

Heads of Ayr Caravan Park, Dunure Road, Ayr, KA7 4LD
☎ *(Alloway) 01292 442269*
8 acres, grassy, level, Mar-Oct, prior booking in peak periods, latest time of arrival 2300.
Extra charge for electricity, awnings.

15 tourers £8.50-11.00 or 5 motors £7.50-9.50 or 5 tents £7.50-9.50.
Total Touring Pitches 20.
10 Holiday Caravans to let, sleep 4-8 £130.00-330.00, total sleeping capacity 60,
min. let 2 nights.

Leisure facilities:
5 mls S of Ayr on A719.

BY AYR, Map Ref. 1G7

MIDDLEMUIR PARK
Tarbolton, near Ayr KA5 5NR
Tel: (01292) 541647   Fax: (01292) 541649

Set in the walled gardens of Montgomery Castle. Superb views, quiet family run.
Ayr, Prestwick, TROON beaches nearby. 25 18-hole golf courses including
Turnberry within 20 miles. New modern high specification holiday homes to rent
or buy. Touring caravans, tents and pets welcome. Children's play area.
Holiday homes from £85 per week. Two or three night breaks from £20 per night.

Touring caravans from £7 per night.
Tents from £5 per night.

Middlemuir Park, Tarbolton, Ayr, Ayrshire, KA5 5NR
☎ *(Tarbolton) 01292 541647 Fax: 01292 541649*
17 acres, grassy, hard-standing, Mar-Oct, prior booking in peak periods, latest
time of arrival 1800, overnight holding area. Extra charge for electricity, awnings.

20 tourers £6.00-8.00 or 20 motors £6.00-8.00 or 20 tents £5.00-7.00.
Total Touring Pitches 20.
25 Holiday Caravans to let, sleep 4-6 £80.00-300.00, total sleeping capacity 125,
min. let 2 nights.

Leisure facilities:
A75 from Dumfries, then A76 Kilmarnock route to Mauchline traffic lights,
turn left onto Ayr rd B743 4 mls on right.

BADACHRO, Ross-shire, Map Ref. 3E7

INSPECTED

Booking Enquiries: Mrs Tallach, 17 Port Henderson, Badachro, by Gairloch,
Ross-shire, IV21 2AS
☎ *(Badachro) 01445 741278 (Mon-Sat)*
Holiday Caravan to let, sleeps 4-5 £100.00-160.00, min.let weekend, Apr-Oct.

BALLANTRAE, Ayrshire, Map Ref. 1F9

Laggan House Leisure Park, Ballantrae, Ayrshire, KA26 0LL
☎ *(Ballantrae) 0146583 229*
28 acres, mixed, Mar-Oct, prior booking in peak periods, latest time of arrival 2200, overnight holding area. Extra charge for electricity, showers.

🔥 🐾 ☉ 🔟 ⚡ 🚰 ⛽ 🚻 E 🆆 🅿 ⟳ ✕ 🏇 🏛 ⚠ ▓ 🛒 ♨ 🎱 🎯 🅣 🆂🅿

10 tourers £6.00-8.00 or 10 motors £6.00-8.00 or 5 tents £4.00-6.00.
Total Touring Pitches 10.
3 Holiday Caravans to let, sleep 6 £140.00-240.00, total sleeping capacity 18, min.let weekend (low season).

🔥 🐾 ☉ 🚻 E 🆆 🅿 ⟳ ✕ 🏇 🏛 ⚠ 🛒 ♨ ▓ 🅣

Leisure facilities: 🏓 🎱 🎣 🎯 🌐
Travelling S on A77 from Ballantrae, take turning left ¼ ml (signposted).
Follow road approx. 3 mls. Park entrance on left.

BALLOCH, Loch Lomond Dunbartonshire, Map Ref. 1H4

tullichewan CARAVAN PARK

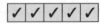

Old Luss Road, Balloch
Loch Lomond G83 8QP
Tel: (01389) 759475   Fax: (01389) 755563

Tullichewan is one of Scotland's finest touring parks. Close to Loch Lomond and Glasgow. Excellent facilities with sheltered, secluded pitches. Superb leisure suite (sauna, jacuzzi, sun-bed), games room, TV lounge, supermarket, launderette, play-area, mountain bike hire. Thistle-Award caravan holiday homes and beautiful pine lodges for hire. Free colour brochure.
Open all year (except November).

Tullichewan Caravan Park, Old Luss Road, Balloch, Loch Lomond, Dunbartonshire, G83 8QP
☎ *(Alexandria) 01389 759475 Fax: 01389 755563*
13½ acres, mixed, Dec-Oct, prior booking in peak periods, latest time of arrival 2200, overnight holding area. Extra charge for electricity, awnings.

🔥 🐾 ☉ 🔟 ⚡ 🚰 ⛽ 🚻 E 🆆 🅿 ♘ ⟳ ✕ 🏇 🏛 ⚠ 🛒 ♨ 🎱 🎯 💱 🅣 🆂🅿

110 tourers £8.50-10.90 or 110 motors £8.50-10.90 or 30 tents £8.50-10.90.
Total Touring Pitches 140.
12 Holiday Caravans to let, sleep 6-8 £150.00-350.00, total sleeping capacity 78, min. let 3 days.

🔥 🐾 ☉ 🚰 🚻 E 🆆 🅿 ♘ ⟳ ✕ 🏇 🏛 ⚠ 🛒 ♨ ▓ 🎯 💱 🅣 🅓

Leisure facilities: 🏓 🎱 ⛵ 🎣 🌐 ▶ 🏊 ⛳ 🔺 🦆 🎿
Turn right off A82 Glasgow-Fort William road, onto A811 at roundabout.
Follow international site signs to Park (½ ml).

VAT is shown at 17.5%: changes in this rate may affect prices.

9

BALMACARA, by Kyle of Lochalsh, Ross-shire, Map Ref. 3F9

Reraig Caravan Site, Balmacara, by Kyle of Lochalsh, Ross-shire, IV40 8DH
☎ *(Balmacara) 0159986 215 (no tel. bookings)*
2 acres, grassy, hard-standing, level, May-Sep, latest time of arrival 2200.
Extra charge for electricity, awnings, showers.

40 tourers £5.80 or 40 motors £5.80 or 5 tents £5.80. Total Touring Pitches 45.
1³/₄ mls (3 km) W junction of A87 and A890 behind Balmacara Hotel.

BALMAHA, by Drymen, Stirlingshire, Map Ref. 1H4

Camping & Caravanning Club Site, Milarrochy Bay, Balmaha, by Drymen, Stirlingshire, G63 0AL
☎ *(Balmaha) 01360 87236*
Booking Enquiries: The Camping & Caravanning Club, Greenfields House, Westwood Way, Coventry, CV4 8JH
☎ *(Coventry) 01203 694995 (out of season) Fax: 01203 694886 (out of season)*
9 acres, grassy, sloping, Mar-Oct, prior booking in peak periods, latest time of arrival 2100, overnight holding area. Extra charge for electricity.

150 tourers £6.73-7.63 or 150 motors £6.73-7.63 or 150 tents £6.73-7.63.
Total Touring Pitches 150.

Leisure facilities: ☻
To Drymen from S, first left to Balmaha look out for right turn up hill. Pass of Balmaha. Road down to Millarochy Bay 1¹/₂ mls from Balmaha. Site on left after cottage on right.

Booking Enquiries: Mrs F MacLuskie, Critreoch, Rowardennan Road, Balmaha, Stirlingshire, G63 0AW
☎ *(Balmaha) 01360 870309*
Holiday Caravan to let, sleeps 4-6 £140.00-155.00, Mar-Oct, min. let 1 week

Leisure facilities: ⌂ ⅄
Take B837 from Drymen. Caravan is at Critreoch, 2 mls beyond Balmaha.

BANCHORY, Kincardineshire, Map Ref. 4F11

Campfield Caravan Site, Glassel, by Banchory, Kincardineshire, AB31 4DN
☎ *(Torphins) 013398 82250*
2 acres, grassy, Apr-Sep, latest time of arrival 2030. Extra charge for electricity, awnings.

4 tourers £5.50-6.50 or 4 motors £5.50-6.50 or 10 tents £5.50-6.50.
Total Touring Pitches 14.
2 Holiday Caravans to let, sleep 4-6 £150.00-166.00, total sleeping capacity 12, min. let weekend.

Leisure facilities: ▶ ∪ ♣
On A980 road, 5 mls N of Banchory.

BANCHORY, Kincardineshire, Map Ref. 4F11

Feughside Caravan Park, Strachan, Banchory, Kincardineshire, AB31 3NT
☎ *(Feughside) 01330 850669*
5 acres, grassy, level, sheltered, Apr-mid Oct, prior booking in peak periods,
latest time of arrival 2000. Extra charge for electricity, awnings.

65

🛠 🐾 ⊙ 🖥 ⚡ 🚿 🚻 P 🧺 ⌖ ✕ 🐎 ⚠ 🛁 ☎ 🕿

20 tourers £7.00-7.50 or 20 motors £7.00-7.50 or 20 tents £5.00-7.50.
Total Touring Pitches 20.
2 Holiday Caravans to let, sleep 6 £125.00-250.00, total sleeping capacity 12,
min. let 1 night.

🛠 🐾 ⊙ 🚿 🚌 E 🚻 P 🧺 ⌖ ✕ 🐎 ⚠ 🛄 🧽 🛢 ♿ Ⓓ

Leisure facilities: 🎱 ✚ 🎣 ♘

From Banchory take B974 (Fettercairn). 3 mls to Strachan. Do not turn left but keep
straight on (B976) for 2 mls to Feughside Inn. Turn right after Inn. Site is 100 yds on.

Silver Ladies Caravan Park, Strachan, Banchory
☎ *(Banchory) 01330 822800*
7.5 acres, grassy, hard-standing, level, Apr-Oct, prior booking in peak periods,
latest time of arrival 2000. Extra charge for electricity, awnings.

103

🛠 🐾 ⊙ 🖥 ⚡ 🚿 🚌 E 🚻 P 🧺 ⌖ ✕ 🐕 🚂 ⚠ 🛁 🛢 🔥 ☎ 🕿 SP

18 tourers £6.25-7.10 or 18 motors £6.25-7.10 or 18 tents £4.90-6.10.
Total Touring Pitches 18.
10 Holiday Caravans to let, sleep 6 £105.00-265.00, total sleeping capacity 60,
min. let 2 nights.

🛠 🐾 ⊙ 🚿 E 🚻 P 🧺 ✕ 🐎 🚂 ⚠ 🛄 🧽 🛢 ♿

Leisure facilities: 🎱 ✚ ♟ 🎣 ♘

BANFF, Map Ref. 4F7

INSPECTED

Banff Links Caravan Park
Booking Enquiries: Mrs C E Reid, 4 Academy Place, Peterhead,
Aberdeenshire, AB42 6JQ
☎ *(Peterhead) 01779 470582*
2 Holiday Caravans to let, sleep 4-8 £120.00-195.00, total sleeping capacity 16,
min. let weekend (low season), Apr-Sep.

Ⓜ 🛠 🐾 ⊙ 🚿 E 🚻 P 🧺 ⌖ ✕ 🐎 🚂 ⚠ 🛄 🧽 🛢 ♿

Leisure facilities: ✚
From Banff take A98 W for 1 ml. Turn right. Signposted 300 yds.

GRADING
YOUR GUARANTEE
OF QUALITY

Key to symbols
is on back flap

VAT is shown at 17.5%: changes in this rate may affect prices.

BEAULY, Inverness-shire, Map Ref. 4A8

✓ ✓ ✓ ✓

🚐 🚐

⛺ 30

🏠 🚐

Cruivend Caravan & Camping Park, Beauly, Inverness-shire, IV4 7BE
☎ *(Beauly) 01463 782367*
3 acres, grassy, hard-standing, level, mid Mar-mid Oct, latest time of arrival 2300, overnight holding area. Extra charge for electricity, awnings, showers.

🔌 📶 ☉ 🗑 ✦ 🍴 🏕 E 🚽 P 🅿 ☮ ✕ 🐕 🚶 ⚠ 🛢 🎡 🛎 ☂ T SP

20 tourers £6.50-8.00 or 20 motors £6.50-8.00 or 20 tents £6.50-8.00.
Total Touring Pitches 20.
5 Holiday Caravans to let, sleep 6 £120.00-250.00, total sleeping capacity 30, min. let 1 night.

🔌 📶 ☉ 🍴 🚪 E 🚽 P 🅿 ☮ ✕ 🐕 🚶 ⚠ 🛄 🖊 🍽 ♨ ☂ T

Leisure facilities: 🎱 ✦ 🏌 ⛳ 🚣 ✓ X

N from Inverness 11 mls on A862, turn first left over Beauly Bridge. 1 ml S of Beauly.

Dunmore House
Beauly, Inverness-shire IV4 7AB   Tel: 01463 782660

At Beauly, near Inverness, three large luxury six berth caravans all with panoramic views over Beauly Firth, Black Isle and hills above Loch Ness, on a quiet croft 1½ miles from village.
All three caravans have lounge, kitchen, bathroom, separate bedrooms, colour TV, fridge. Central for touring highlands.
Pets welcome.

INSPECTED

Booking Enquiries: Mrs J Aiton, Dunmore House, Beauly, Inverness-shire, IV4 7AB
☎ *(Beauly) 01463 782660*
3 Holiday Caravans to let, sleep 6 £93.00-178.00, total sleeping capacity 18, min.let 1 night, Apr-Oct.

🔌 📶 🚪 🍴 E 🚽 P 🅿 ✕ 🐕 ⚠ 🎡 🍽 ♨ 🎣

Leisure facilities: 🏌
From Inverness take A862 to Beauly, turn left at Bank of Scotland, up lane, straight across crossroads to top of hill. Turn right. Caravans 500 yds on right.

BIGGAR, Lanarkshire, Map Ref. 2C6

✓ ✓ ✓ ✓

🚐

12

🚐

Biggar Caravan Site, Biggar Park, Biggar, Lanarkshire, ML12 6JS
☎ *(Biggar) 01899 20319*
6 acres, grassy, stony, Apr-Oct, prior booking in peak periods, latest time of arrival 2000, restricted to Caravan Club. Extra charge for awnings.

🔌 📶 ☉ 🗑 🍴 🚽 P 🅿 ☮ ✕ 🐕 ⚠ 🍽 🎱 🛢 🎵 🔔

12 tourers £6.70-7.50 or 12 motors £6.70-7.50. Total Touring Pitches 12. No tents.
Leisure facilities: 🎿 🏌 🛷
From Biggar, take B7016 Broughton road on NE of Biggar for about 200 yds on to unclassified road for Park.

BLACKBURN, West Lothian, Map Ref. 2B5

✓ ✓ ✓

🚐

⛺ 25

🚐

Mosshall Farm, Blackburn, West Lothian, EH49
☎ *(Blackburn) 01501 762318*
¾ acres, mixed, Jan-Dec, latest time of arrival 1800, overnight holding area.

Extra charge for electricity, awnings, showers.

📶 ☉ E 🚽 P 🅿 ✕ 🐕 🎱 🛢 🍴 🔔 D

15 tourers £4.00-5.00 or 15 motors £4.00-5.00 or 15 tents £4.00-5.00. Total Touring Pitches 15.
Leave M8 junc.4. Take road for Whitburn at T junction (A705).
Turn left ½ ml on right.

BLACKWOOD, Lanarkshire, Map Ref. 2A6

INSPECTED

Mrs J Stewart, Draffan, Marshill Farm, Blackwood, Lesmahagow, Lanarkshire, ML11 9PW
☎ *(Lesmahagow) 01555 860257*
1 acre, grassy, level, sheltered, Apr-Oct, latest time of arrival 22.00.
Extra charge for electricity, awnings.
🔥 🐾 ☉ E wc P 🛒 ✕ 🐕 🏔 ⚱ 🕃 📞
10 tourers from £5.00 or 10 motors from £5.00 or 10 tents from £4.00. Total touring pitches 10.
Holiday Caravan to let, sleeps 4-6 £105.00.
🏔 🎣
Leisure facilities: 🎣 ✪ ► ◢ ∪ 💧
M74 leave at junction 8. Take B7078 to Blackwood, travel 3 mls, turn left at
Craigrethan Castle, Draffan sign. Farm first left (½ ml).

BLAIR ATHOLL, Perthshire, Map Ref. 4C12

BLAIR CASTLE CARAVAN PARK
BLAIR ATHOLL, PERTHSHIRE PH18 5SR
Telephone: (01796) 481263 Fax: (01796) 481587

Have an unforgettable holiday in Highland Perthshire in one of our
fully equipped luxury caravan holiday homes. All caravans are fully
serviced with all mod cons, kitchen, shower room, lounge and up to
three bedrooms. Mains-serviced touring pitches also available.
Fishing, golf, pony trekking, mountain bikes available.

Blair Castle Caravan Park, Blair Atholl, Perthshire, PH18 5SR
☎ *(Blair Atholl) 01796 481263 Fax: 01796 481587*
32 acres, mixed, Apr-Oct, prior booking in peak periods, latest time of arrival 2130,
overnight holding area. Extra charge for electricity, awnings.
🔥 🐾 ☉ 🖥 ✍ 🚗 🏧 ⛺ E wc P 🕃 ✕ 🐕 🏛 🏔 R 🛁 ⚒ 🕃 📞 🍴 ⌖
144 tourers £8.00-9.00 or 15 motors £8.00-9.00 or 82 tents £5.50-6.50.
Total Touring Pitches 241.
27 Holiday Caravans to let, sleep 2-6 £130.00-295.00, total sleeping capacity 140,
min. let 3 nights.
🔥 🐾 ☉ ⛺ E wc P ✕ 🐕 🏛 🏔 🚽 ⚒ 📀 🔒 🕃 ⌖ D
Leisure facilities: 🎣 ✪ ► ◢ ∪
Take A9 N from Pitlochry. Turn off for Blair Atholl after 6 mls.

THE RIVER TILT CARAVAN PARK
Blair Atholl, by Pitlochry, Perthshire PH18 5TE
Telephone: 01796 481467 Fax: 01796 481511

This rather nice park in a unique location between the golf course and
delightful 'River Tilt' amidst magnificent scenery. Awarded Best Park
In Scotland 1993. Facilities include indoor pool/gym complex.
Overlooked by 'The Loft' Award winning restaurant, tennis, activity
play area, fully serviced touring pitches, new heated shower block.
New for '95 – luxury caravans overlooking the river for holiday hire.

River Tilt Caravan Park, Blair Atholl, by Pitlochry, Perthshire, PH18 5TE
☎ *(Blair Atholl) 01796 481467 Fax: 01796 481511*
14 acres, grassy, hard-standing, level, Apr-Oct, prior booking in peak periods,
latest time of arrival 1800. Extra charge for electricity, awnings, showers.
🔥 🐾 🚐 ☉ 🖥 ✍ 🚗 🏧 E wc P 🛒 🕃 ✕ 🏛 🏔 R 🕃 ⚱ 📞 🕃 T
40 tourers £12.00 or 40 motors £11.00 or 40 tents £12.00. Total Touring Pitches 45.
5 Holiday Caravans to let, sleep 4-6 £250.00-300.00, total sleeping capacity 30.
🔥 🐾 🚐 ☉ 🚗 ⛺ E wc P 🛒 🕃 ✕ 🏛 🏔 📀 📀 🔒 🕃 T D
Leisure facilities: 🏊 ♨ 🎱 ⛳ ✪ 🎾 ► ◢ ∪ ✓ 🎯 💧 ⚓ 🎣 ⚓
Turn off A9 N of Pitlochry (signposted Blair Atholl B8079).
As you arrive in Blair Atholl, turn sharp left at the Tilt Hotel.

Key to symbols
is on back flap

VAT is shown at 17.5%: changes in this rate may affect prices.

13

BLAIRGOWRIE, Perthshire, Map Ref. 2C1

Blairgowrie Caravan Park

RATTRAY, BLAIRGOWRIE, PERTHSHIRE PH10 7AL
Telephone: (01250) 872941   Fax No: (01250) 874535

Thistle award-winning Caravan Holiday Homes and Pine Lodges available for hire on this beautifully landscaped park adjoining Blairgowrie. Park facilities include licensed supermarket, launderette, adventure playground, putting green, paddling pool, cycle hire. Tourers welcome. OPEN ALL YEAR. Golf, indoor heated swimming pool, fishing, riding locally; skiing nearby. Short breaks available.

Prices: £95-£325 per week. Tourers £7-£8 per night

Blairgowrie Caravan Park, Rattray, Blairgowrie, Perthshire, PH10 7AL
☎ *(Blairgowrie) 01250 872941 Fax: 01250 874535*
15 acres, grassy, level, sheltered, Jan-Oct, prior booking in peak periods, latest time of arrival 2000. Extra charge for electricity, awnings.

30 tourers £7.00-8.00 or 5 motors £6.00-7.00 or 15 tents £7.00-8.00.
Total Touring Pitches 30.
20 Holiday Caravans to let, sleep 4-8 £100.00-320.00, total sleeping capacity 120, min. let 2 nights.

Leisure facilities:
¹/₂ ml N of Blairgowrie town centre off A93 Braemar road, turn right at signpost.

BOAT OF GARTEN, Inverness-shire, Map Ref. 4C10

Campgrounds of Scotland, Boat of Garten, Inverness-shire, PH24
☎ *(Boat of Garten) 01479 831652 Fax: 01479 831652*
6 acres, mixed, Jan-Dec, prior booking in peak periods, latest time of arrival 2200, overnight holding area. Extra charge for electricity, awnings.

37 tourers from £5.50 or 37 motors from £5.50 or 37 tents from £4.50.
Total Touring Pitches 37.
5 Holiday Caravans to let, sleep 4-6 from £170.00, total sleeping capacity 28, min. let 2 nights.

Leisure facilities:
In village of Boat of Garten, 5 mls N of Aviemore.

Croftnacarn Caravan Park, Loch Garten Road, Boat of Garten

☎ *(Boat of Garten) 01309 672051 Fax: 01309 676860*
3 acres, grassy, level, sheltered, Dec-Oct, prior booking in peak periods, latest time of arrival 1900. Extra charge for electricity, awnings.

5 tourers £5.00-7.00 or 5 motors £5.00-7.00 or 5 tents £3.00-7.00.
Total Touring Pitches 5.
7 Holiday Caravans to let, sleep 6 £55.00-250.00, total sleeping capacity 42, min. let 2 nights (low season).

Leisure facilities:
1 ml from Boat of Garten on Loch Garten road.

Important: Prices stated are estimates and may be subject to amendments

BRIDGE OF CALLY, Perthshire, Map Ref. 2C1

Corriefodly Holiday Park, Bridge of Cally, Perthshire, PH10 7JG
☎ *(Bridge of Cally) 01250 886236*
5 acres, grassy, sloping, sheltered, Dec-Oct, prior booking in peak periods, latest time of arrival 2300, overnight holding area. Extra charge for electricity, awnings, showers.

38 tourers £6.50-8.50 or 38 motors £6.50-8.50 or 38 tents £5.00-7.00.
Total Touring Pitches 38.
Leisure facilities:
From Blairgowrie take A93 N for 6 mls to Bridge of Cally. Cross over bridge, turn left on A924 for 300 yds.

BY BROUGHTON, Peeebleshire, Map Ref. 2C6

Booking Enquiries: Easter Calzeat, Broughton, by Biggar, Lanarkshire, ML12 6HQ
☎ *(Broughton) 018994 359*
2 Holiday Caravans to let, sleep 4-6 £100.00-140.00, total sleeping capacity 12, min. let 2 nights. Apr-Oct.

Leisure facilities:
Off A701 at war memorial, follow road along Biggar Water, past bowling green to Site (approx. ¼ ml).

CALLANDER Perthshire, Map Ref. 2A3

Callander Holiday Park, Invertrossachs Road, Callander, Perthshire, FK17 8HW
☎ *(Callander) 01877 330265*
36 acres, hard-standing, level, sheltered, Mar-Oct, latest time of arrival 2200, overnight holding area. Extra charge for electricity, awnings.

54 tourers £10.00 or 54 motors £10.00. Total Touring Pitches 54. No tents.
Leisure facilities:
Signposted from A81 (Callander-Glasgow).

QUALITY
AT ITS BEST.
THISTLE AWARD

Key to symbols is on back flap

VAT is shown at 17.5%: changes in this rate may affect prices.

CALLANDER, Perthshire, Map Ref. 2A3

**Cambusmore Estate, Auchenlaich Caravan Park, Callander,
Perthshire, FK17 8LQ**
☎ *(Callander) 01877 330811*
4 acres, grassy, sloping, sheltered, Apr-Oct. Extra charge for electricity, awnings, showers.

🔧 🐾 ☉ E ⓦⓒ Ⓟ 🦮 ✕ 🔥 ⛽

20 tourers £6.00 or 20 motors £6.00 or 30 tents £6.00. Total Touring Pitches 30.
On A84 between Doune and Callander near Heather Centre.

Gart Caravan Park, Callander, Perthshire, FK17
☎ *(Callander) 01877 30002*
25 acres, grassy, level, sheltered, Easter-mid Oct, prior booking in peak periods,
latest time of arrival 2200, overnight holding area. Extra charge for electricity, awnings.

🔧 🐾 ☉ 🗑 ⚡ ⚓ 🏪 E ⓦⓒ Ⓟ 🦮 ♿ ✕ 🐎 🏍 🔥 ⛽ 🐕 Ⓓ

121 tourers £10.00-10.50 or 121 motors £10.00-10.50. Total Touring Pitches 121.
No tents.
Leisure facilities: 🎱 ♪ ♨
On A84 between Callander and Doune.

CARRADALE, Argyll, Map Ref. 1E7

CARRADALE CHALETS
**Carradale Bay Caravan Park, Carradale, Kintyre, Argyll PA28 6QG
Telephone: 01583 431665**
*New comfortably furnished pinelog chalets sleep 4/5 with beautiful
views across to the hills of Arran. Our spacious park is bounded by
the River Carra on a safe sandy beach. Excellent opportunities for
boat launching, fishing, walking and canoeing. From £150 per week.*
We also welcome touring caravans and tents.

Carradale Bay Caravan Site, Carradale Bay, Carradale, Argyll, PA28 6QG
☎ *(Carradale) 01583 431665*
Booking Enquiries: Ranworth, 45 Eastgate, Hornsea,
North Humberside, HU18 1LP
☎ *(Hornsea) 01964 533766*
9 acres, mixed, Easter-Sep, prior booking in peak periods, latest time of arrival 2200,
overnight holding area. Extra charge for electricity.

🔧 🐾 ☉ 🗑 ⚡ ⚓ 🏪 E ⓦⓒ Ⓟ 🦮 ♿ ✕ 🐎 🏍 🔥 ⛽

60 tourers £5.40-8.20 or 60 motors £5.40-8.20 or 60 tents £5.40-8.20.
Total Touring Pitches 60.
3 Holiday Caravans to let, sleep 4-5 £150.00-300.00, total sleeping capacity 14,
min. let 4 nights.

Ⓜ 🔧 🐾 ⚓ ☉ ⚓ 🏠 E ⓦⓒ Ⓟ 🦮 ♿ ✕ 🐎 🏍 🔥 🏠 ◎ 🍴 ⛱

Leisure facilities: 🎱 ♨
Take A82 from Glasgow, then A83 at Tarbet to Tarbert (Loch Fyne).
Continue S and take B8001/B842 to Carradale. Turn right into Carradale village
and Site is on the right.

COCKBURNSPATH, Berwickshire, Map Ref. 2F5

302

Pease Bay Caravan Park, Cockburnspath, Berwickshire, TD13 5YP
☎ *(Cockburnspath) 01368 830206 Fax: 01368 830663*
18 acres, mixed, Apr-Oct, prior booking in peak periods, latest time of arrival 2100.
Extra charge for electricity, awnings, showers.

🔧🐾🛒☉🗑✂🚗🛖🚻Ｅ🆆🅿☦✕🔦⛺⚠🍴🅡🛎🚿⚓🎵🔌📞💷

12 tourers £6.00-8.00 or 12 motors £6.00-8.00 or 12 tents £5.00-7.00.
Total Touring Pitches 12.

Leisure facilities: ✪
Eight mls S of Dunbar on A1, road on left, 22 mls N of Berwick-on-Tweed on A1 on right.

COLDINGHAM, Berwickshire, Map Ref. 2F5

175

Coldingham Caravan Park, Coldingham, Berwickshire, TD14
☎ *(Coldingham) 018907 71316*
Booking Enquiries: Rodger Fish & Son Ltd, Shedden Park Road, Kelso,
Roxburghshire, TD5 7AL
☎ *(Kelso) 01573 224488 Fax: 01573 226410*
10 acres, mixed, Mar-Nov, latest time of arrival 2300. Extra charge for electricity,
awnings, showers.

🔧🐾☉🗑✂🚻Ｅ🅿☦✕🔦🍴⚓📞🅳

25 tourers £5.50 and 4 motors £5.50. Total Touring Pitches 29. No tents.
From north leave A1, join A1107. From south leave A1, join B6438.
Turn left in Coldingham ('/4 ml).

TELEPHONE DIALLING CODES

On 16 April 1995 all UK area codes starting **0** will start **01**.

From August 1994 until 16 April 1995, the new codes will be run in parallel with the old ones.
If you experience difficulty in connecting a call, please call Directory Enquiries – **192** – for advice. Please note: A charge will be made for this service when using a private phone.

Key to symbols
is on back flap

VAT is shown at 17.5%: changes in this rate may affect prices.

COLDINGHAM, Berwickshire, Map Ref. 2F5

Scoutscroft Holiday Centre, Coldingham, Berwickshire, TD14 5NB
☎ *(Coldingham) 018907 71338/71534 Fax: 018907 71747*
10 acres, grassy, sheltered, Mar-Nov, prior booking in peak periods,
latest time of arrival 2400. Extra charge for electricity, awnings.

🔥 ⚡☉回✻ 🍴⬛□E ⬛P♿↻✗🐴⚠️♨️Ⓡ🛒♨️⚡🐾🅰️

30 tourers £7.00-8.00 or 30 motors £7.00-8.00 or 60 tents £7.00-8.00.
Total Touring Pitches 60.
10 Holiday Caravans to let, sleep 6 £100.00-220.00, total sleeping capacity 60,
min. let 2 nights.

🔥 ⚡🚲□E⬛P♿↻✗🐴⚠️🏠🪣🚿🐾🅰️

Leisure facilities: ⚓▶🏊⛳🛶
12 mls N of Berwick-on-Tweed. Turn N off A1 at Reston-Coldingham.
Site on St Abbs side of Coldingham village.

COMRIE, Perthshire, Map Ref. 2A2

Riverside Caravan Park, Old Station Road, Comrie, Perthshire, PH6 2EA
☎ *(Comrie) 01764 670555/670207*
7 acres, grassy, Apr-Oct, prior booking in peak periods, latest time of arrival 2000.
Extra charge for electricity, awnings.

🔥 ⚡🚲☉回✻ 🍴⬛E⬛P↻🐴⚠️♨️⚡🐾

5 tourers £9.00 or 5 motors £9.00. Total Touring Pitches 20. No tents.
6 Holiday Caravans to let, sleep 4-6 £170.00-215.00, total sleeping capacity 36.

🔥 ⚡🚲□E⬛P↻⚠️🪣🚿

On the A85 – S side – in village of Comrie, 7 mls from Crieff.

Twenty Shilling Wood Caravan Park, Comrie, Perthshire, PH6 2JY
☎ *(Comrie) 01764 670411*
10 acres, mixed, Mar-Oct, prior booking in peak periods, latest time of arrival 2100,
overnight holding area. Extra charge for electricity, awnings, showers.

🔥 ⚡☉回✻ 🍴⬛E⬛P♿↻✗🐴♨️⚡🐾

25 tourers £6.00-8.00 or 25 motors £6.00-8.00. Total Touring Pitches 25. No tents.
2 Holiday Caravans to let, sleep 2-4 £110.00-245.00, total sleeping capacity 8,
min. let 1 week.

🔥 ⚡□E⬛P♿↻✗🏠🪣🚿

Leisure facilities: ⚓🔱
¹/₂ ml W of Comrie on A85 opposite Farm Food Bar.

INSPECTED

Booking Enquiries: Mrs P Booth, Lochview Farm, Mill of Fortune, Comrie,
Perthshire, PH6 2JE
☎ *(Comrie) 01764 670677*
2 Holiday Caravans to let, sleep 4 £90.00-190.00, total sleeping capacity 8,
min. let 4 days, Apr-Oct.

🔥 ⚡🚲☉⬛□E⬛P♿✗🐴🏠🪣🚿🪣⛸️

Leisure facilities: 🔱🏃‍♂️🎣▶🏊
A85 to Comrie, turn at Braco turn off in centre of Comrie. About 2 mls turn left at
Glascorrie Road, then first left up to Loch View Farm.

CONNEL, Argyll, Map Ref. 1E2

Camping & Caravanning Club Site, Barcaldine, by Connel, Arygll, PA37 1SG
☎ (Ledaig) 0163172 348
Booking Enquiries: Camping & Caravanning Club, Greenfields House,
Westwood Way, Coventry, CV4 8JH
☎ (Coventry) 01203 694995 Fax: 01203 694886
6 acres, mixed, Mar-Oct, prior booking in peak periods, latest time of arrival 2100,
overnight holding area. Extra charge for electricity.

🔧 🕯 ☉ 🗑 ⚡ 🚿 📶 E 🚾 🅿 🔄 ✖ 🏇 ⚠ 🍴 🅁 🚰 ⚴ 🐾 🔧 £

75 tourers £6.62-7.41 or 75 motors £6.62-7.41 or 75 tents £6.62-7.41.
Total Touring Pitches 75.

Leisure facilities: 🔍
A828 Oban-Fort William road approx. 6 mls N of Connel Bridge.

BY CRAIGELLACHIE, Banffshire, Map Ref. 4D8

Camping & Caravanning Club Site Speyside, Elchies, Craigellachie, Aberlour,
Banffshire, AB38 9SD
☎ (Carron) 01340 810414
Booking Enquiries: The Camping & Caravanning Club, Greenfields House,
Westwood Way, Coventry, CV4 8JH
☎ (Coventry) 01203 694995 Fax: 01203 694886
3 acres, mixed, Mar-Oct, prior booking in peak periods, latest time of arrival 2100.
Extra charge for electricity.

🔧 🕯 ☉ 🗑 🚿 📶 E 🚾 🅿 🔄 ✖ 🐕 🍴 🐾 🔧 £

25 tourers £6.62-7.41 or 25 motors £6.62-7.41 or 25 tents £6.62-7.41.
Total Touring Pitches 25.

Leisure facilities: 🏴 ⚓ ⛵ ∪
Situated on B9102 2½ mls from junction with A941 Elgin-Craigellachie road.

Key to symbols
is on back flap

VAT is shown at 17.5%: changes in this rate may affect prices.

CRAIGNURE, Isle of Mull, Argyll, Map Ref. 1D2

ISLE OF MULL

THIS IS A SHIELING - one of 12 unique carpeted cottage tents (4 with kitchen and bathroom) spaced in 3 glorious acres by the sea. Each has this view of Ben Nevis.
A SHIELING HOLIDAY INCLUDES:
FREE ACTIVITIES - water sports, fishing, expeditions, painting etc.
FREE FACILITIES - spotless, with constant hot water. Shingle beach, pier and slip. Payphone. Laundry. Stroll to ferry, shop, cafe, pub, steam railway and buses for Iona (for Staffa) and Tobermory (for Coll and Tiree). Walk to golf, and Torosay and Duart Castles.
1995 PRICE: FROM £35 PER PERSON PER WEEK. Great value, as the Shieling's a great idea - 10 successful years.
FREE colour brochure with guarantee:
David and Moira Gracie, Shieling Holidays (2), Craignure, Isle of Mull PA65 6AY.
Telephone: 01680-812496.
PS: separate touring facilities ✓ ✓ ✓ ✓ see below.
AA: "3 pennants; one of Britain's best sites; environment award".

David Gracie, Shieling Holidays, Craignure, Isle of Mull, Argyll, PA65 6AY
☎ *(Craignure)* 01680 812496
7 acres, mixed, Apr-Oct, prior booking in peak periods, latest time of arrival 2200, overnight holding area. Extra charge for electricity, awnings.

30 tourers from £8.50 or 30 motors from £8.50 or 30 tents from £8.50. Total Touring Pitches 60.

Leisure facilities: ● ⊕ ⊢ ♪ ♫ ∪ ♦ ♣ ⚓

From ferry pier at Craignure turn S on A849 (Bunessan). In about ¼ ml by church turn left into lane past old pier to Site.

Alex MacFadyen, Balmeanach Park, Craignure, Fishnish, Isle of Mull, Argyll
☎ *(Aros)* 01680 300342
1 acre, grassy, hard-standing, Mar-Oct, prior booking in peak periods, latest time of arrival 2100, overnight holding area. Extra charge for awnings.

2 tourers £6.00 or 2 motors £6.00 or 10 tents £6.00. Total Touring Pitches 12.
Leisure facilities: ⊢ ♪ ♫ ∪ ♦ ♣
From Craignure take A849 N 5 mls. 100 mtrs. past Lochaline ferry road.

Important: Prices stated are estimates and may be subject to amendments

CREETOWN, Wigtownshire, Map Ref. 1H10

Castle Cary Holiday Park, Creetown, Wigtownshire, DG8 7DQ
☎ *(Creetown) 01671 820264*
16 acres, mixed, Easter-Oct, latest time of arrival 2200, overnight holding area.
Extra charge for electricity, awnings.

🔥 🏕 ➡ ☉ 🗑 ⚡ 🚱 🏕 ⌨ E 🚾 P 🅿 ♿ ✕ 🐴 ⚠ 🍴 Ⓡ 🛒 ♿ ⚴ 🔌 🅿 ⚡

55 tourers £6.80-9.00 or 55 motors £6.80-9.00 or 55 tents £6.80-9.00.
Total Touring Pitches 55.
3 Holiday Caravans to let, sleep 4-6 £125.00-166.00, total sleeping capacity 18,
min. let 3 nights.

🔥 🏕 ➡ 🚱 ⌨ E 🚾 P 🅿 ♿ ✕ 🐴 ⚠ ⬭ 🗑 ⚴ † 🅿 Ⓓ

Leisure facilities: 🎱 ⚓ ⚓ 🎣 ☀ 🎿
Half mile S of Creetown village, lodge gate entrance clearly visible, on main A75 trunk road.

Creetown Caravan Park, Silver Street, Creetown, Wigtownshire, DG8 7HU
☎ *(Creetown) 01671 820377*
3 acres, grassy, level, Mar-Oct, latest time of arrival 2230. Extra charge for showers.

🔥 🏕 ➡ ☉ 🗑 ⚡ 🚱 ⌨ E 🚾 P 🅿 ♿ ✕ 🐴 ⚠ ⬭ 🍴 🅿 Ⓣ ⓢ🅿

10 tourers £7.50-8.50 or 10 motors £7.50-8.50 or 10 tents £7.50-8.50.
Total Touring Pitches 20.
7 Holiday Caravans to let, sleep 4-6 £95.00-225.00, total sleeping capacity 42,
min. let 1 day.

🔥 🏕 ☉ ⌨ E 🚾 P 🅿 ♿ ✕ 🐴 ⚠ ⚴ 🗑 ⚴ Ⓣ Ⓓ

Leisure facilities: ⚓ ⚓ ☀
Turn off A75 6 mls E of Newton Stewart into village of Creetown.

CRIANLARICH, Perthshire, Map Ref. 1G2

Glendochart Caravan Park, Glendochart, by Crianlarich, Perthshire, FK20 8QT
☎ *(Killin) 01567 820637*
15 acres, mixed, Mar-Oct, prior booking in peak periods, latest time of arrival 2200,
overnight holding area. Extra charge for electricity, awnings, showers.

🔥 🏕 ☉ 🗑 ⚡ 🚱 ⌨ E 🚾 P ♿ ✕ 🐴 ⚠ ⚴ ♿ 🔌 🅿

45 tourers £6.50-7.50 or 45 motors £6.50-7.50 or 10 tents £6.50-7.50.
Total Touring Pitches 45.
2 Holiday Caravans to let, sleep 1-4 £170.00-220.00, total sleeping capacity 8,
min. let 1 week.

🔥 🏕 ☉ ⌨ E 🚾 P ♿ ✕ 🐴 ⚠ ⚴ 🗑 ⚴

Leisure facilities: ☀ ▶ 🎿 ∪ ✓ ☒ ⛰ ⚘ ⛵ ⚓
On A85 Lochearnhead-Crianlarich road. 5 mls W past A827 turn-off to Killin.

GRADING
YOUR GUARANTEE
OF QUALITY

Key to symbols
is on back flap

VAT is shown at 17.5%: changes in this rate may affect prices.

21

CRIEFF, Perthshire, Map Ref. 2B2

Braidhaugh Caravan Park Ltd, South Bridgend, Crieff, Perthshire, PH7 4HP
☎ *(Crieff) 01764 652951 Fax: 01764 652692*
4³/₄ acres, hard-standing, level, Jan-Dec, prior booking in peak periods, latest time of arrival 2100, overnight holding area. Extra charge for electricity, awnings.

30 tourers £7.00-8.50 or 30 motors £7.00-8.50. Total Touring Pitches 30. No tents.
7 Holiday Caravans to let, sleep 4-7 £125.00-295.00, total sleeping capacity 36, min. let 1 night (low season).

Leisure facilities: ● ● ▶ ✦ ∪ ▲ ● ⤢
From Stirling take A822 to Crieff. 300 yds past Visitor Centre on left. From Perth take A85 to Crieff straight through the town, then left onto A822 to Stirling. Immediately over bridge on right.

Crieff Holiday Village, Turret Bank, Crieff, Perthshire, PH7 4JN
☎ *(Crieff) 01764 3513/653513*
Booking Enquiries: D M & C P T Sloan
4 acres, mixed, Jan-Dec, prior booking in peak periods, latest time of arrival 2400, overnight holding area. Extra charge for electricity, awnings.

36 tourers £7.15-8.50 or 36 motors £7.15-8.50 or 10 tents £6.00-7.00.
Total Touring Pitches 36.
5 Holiday Caravans to let, sleep 4-6 £135.00-250.00, total sleeping capacity 30, min. let 2 nights.

Leisure facilities: ● ▶ ✦ ∪
Follow A85 Crieff-Comrie road, turn left ¹/₄ ml from Crieff at first crossroads. Site 300 yds on left.

CRINAN, Argyll, Map Ref. 1E4

Booking Enquiries: Mrs Anderson, Tigh Na Glaic, Crinan, by Lochgilphead, Argyll, PA31 8SW
☎ *(Crinan) 0154683 245*
Holiday Caravan to let, sleeps 2-6 £100.00-160.00, min. let 1 night, Jan-Dec.

Leisure facilities: ✦ ▶ ✦ ✦ ∪ ▲ ✦

CROCKETFORD, Kirkcudbrightshire, Map Ref. 2B10

PARK OF BRANDEDLEYS
Crocketford, by Dumfries

Practical Caravan's Regional Choice 1993, a family park enjoying a prime situation with extensive fine views over loch and hill. Historic buildings, gardens, museums, shops, beaches, fishing, walks and golf within easy reach, provide the ingredients for a super holiday. An intimate small bar and restaurant adjoins the indoor swimming pool and sauna. The outdoor pool, tennis courts, badminton court, putting course, golf net, games room and play areas complement the excellent toilets and laundries.
Luxury holiday caravans to let.

Resident Proprietors: A & M McDonald.
Telephone: Crocketford 01556 690250.
Fax: 01556 690681.

Park of Brandedleys, Crocketford, by Dumfries, DG2 8RG
☎ *(Crocketford) 01556 690250 Fax: 01556 690681*
Booking Enquiries: A W & M M S McDonald, Park of Brandedleys, Crocketford, by Dumfries
☎ *(Crocketford) 01556 690250 Fax: 01556 690681*
24 acres, mixed, Mar-Oct, prior booking in peak periods, latest time of arrival 2200, overnight holding area. Extra charge for electricity, awnings.

80 tourers £9.00-12.50 or 80 motors £9.00-12.50 or 80 tents £9.00-12.50.
Total Touring Pitches 80.
12 Holiday Caravans to let, sleep 2-8 £125.00-350.00, total sleeping capacity 76, min. let 3 days.

Leisure facilities:
From Dumfries take A75 W for 9 mls. Turn left onto unclassified road on leaving Crocketford village. Park is 150 yds on right

---

BY CROY Inverness-shire, Map Ref. 4B8

Booking Enquiries: Mrs J Douglas, Little Dalcross, Croy, Inverness, Inverness-shire, IV1 2PS
☎ *(Croy) 01667 483224*
Holiday Caravan to let, sleeps 4-6 £80.00-115.00, Apr-Oct.

WELCOME
Whenever you are in Scotland, you can be sure of a warm welcome at your nearest Tourist Information Centre.
For guide books, maps, souvenirs, our Centres provide a service second to none – many now offer bureau-de-change facilities. And, of course, Tourist Information Centres offer free, expert advice on what to see and do, route-planning and accommodation for everyone – visitors and residents alike!

Key to symbols
is on back flap

CUMNOCK, Ayrshire, Map Ref. 2A7

Woodroad Park Caravan & Camping Site, Cumnock, Ayrshire, KA18 3JQ
☎ *(Cumnock) 01290 422111*
Booking Enquiries: Parks Department, Council Offices, Cumnock and
Doon Valley District Council, Lugar, by Cumnock, Ayrshire, KA18 3JQ
☎ *(Cumnock) 01290 422111*
6 acres, grassy, Apr-Sep, overnight holding area. Extra charge for electricity, awnings.

🔦 🜲 ⊙ 🔲 ✂ 🍳 🌭 E 🄿 🄳 ✕ 🐎 🛖 Ⓡ ⚱ 😃 🎯

100 tourers from £5.10 or 100 motors from £5.10 or 100 tents from £5.10.
Total Touring Pitches 200.
Leisure facilities: 🎿 🜨 🎾
Within Cumnock on A76.

CUPAR, Fife, Map Ref. 2D3

INSPECTED

Booking Enquiries: J G Lang & Son, Hilton of Carslogie, Cupar, Fife, KY15 4NG
☎ *(Cupar) 01334 52113*
2 Holiday Caravans to let, sleep 6 from £105.00, total sleeping capacity 12,
min. let weekend, Apr-Oct.

🔦 🜲 🄳 E 🅆🄲 🄿 🛒 ✕ 🐎 🛏 🛖 🍳 ✂ 🍽 🔥 🌿 🎯

2 mls W of Cupar on A91, opposite Scotts Porridge Oats factory.

TELEPHONE DIALLING CODES

On 16 April 1995 all UK area codes starting **0** will start **01**.

From August 1994 until 16 April 1995, the new codes will be run in parallel with the old ones.
If you experience difficulty in connecting a call, please call Directory Enquiries – **192** – for advice. Please note: A charge will be made for this service when using a private phone.

DALKEITH, Midlothian, Map Ref. 2D5

FORDEL CARAVAN AND CAMPING PARK
Fordel, Lauder Road, Dalkeith, Midlothian EH22 2PH
Telephone: 0131-660 3921   0131-663 3046 (24 hours)
Fordel Park is your secluded country retreat. But more than that, its situation just eight miles south of Edinburgh (on the A68 Edinburgh-Newcastle road) makes it the perfect base for exploring Scotland's capital city and the surrounding countryside with Edinburgh's bypass a few minutes drive.

45

Fordel Caravan and Camping Park, Lauder Road, Dalkeith, Midlothian, EH22 2PH
☎ *0131 663 3046 (24hrs)/660 3921 (9am-5pm)*
5 acres, mixed, Mar-Oct, prior booking in peak periods. Extra charge for electricity, showers.

🔧 ⛺ ☉ 🚿 🏕 E 📶 P ⚙ ✕ 🏇 ⚠ 🍴 Ⓡ 🎿 ♿ 🛢 🔌 ☎ ✂ £

45 tourers £7.00-8.50 or 45 motors £7.00-8.50 or 45 tents from £6.00.
Total Touring Pitches 45.

Leisure facilities: ▶
2 mls S of Dalkeith on A68 Edinburgh to Newcastle. 9 mls S of Edinburgh.

DAVIOT, Inverness-shire, Map Ref. 4B9

AUCHNAHILLIN CARAVAN & CAMPING PARK
Daviot (East), Inverness, Inverness-shire IV1 2XQ
Telephone: (01463) 772286   Fax: (01463) 772286
Superb range of luxury caravans in a peaceful location only 5 minutes from Inverness and 20 minutes from Aviemore. Ideal base for touring the Highlands. Excellent site amenities. Bar, restaurant, shop etc on site. Tourers and campers welcome.
STATICS from **£60** for three nights.
TOURERS from **£6.75** per night.

100

Auchnahillin Caravan & Camping Park, Daviot (East), Inverness, Inverness-shire, IV1 2XQ
☎ *(Inverness) 01463 772286 Fax: 01463 772286*
10 acres, grassy, hard-standing, level, Mar-Oct, prior booking in peak periods, latest time of arrival 2200, overnight holding area. Extra charge for electricity, awnings, showers.

🔧 ⛺ ☉ 🛢 🚿 🏕 E 📶 P ⚙ ✕ 🏇 🏨 ⚠ 🍴 Ⓡ 🎿 ♿ 🛢 🎵 🔌 ☎ ✂ Ⓣ SP

45 tourers £6.75-8.50 or 45 motors £6.75-8.50 or 20 tents £5.50-7.50.
Total Touring Pitches 65.
18 Holiday Caravans to let, sleep 4-8 £90.00-300.00, total sleeping capacity 104, min. let 2 nights.

Ⓜ 🔧 ⛺ ➕ ☉ 🏕 🖥 E 📶 P ⚙ 🏇 🏨 ⚠ 🛢 🔌 🛢 ✂ Ⓣ

Leisure facilities: ♣ ▶ 🎣 🥏 ∪ ╱ ⛰ ⚓
Situated 7 mls SE of Inverness on B9154 (Moy road) off A9.

DIABAIG, Torridon Ross-shire, Map Ref. 3F8

INSPECTED

Booking Enquiries: Miss I A Ross, 3 Diabaig, Torridon, Achnasheen, Ross-shire, IV22 2HE
☎ *(Diabaig) 01445 790240/790268*
Holiday Caravan to let, sleeps 4-5 from £75.00, min.let 1 night, Jan-Dec.

Ⓜ 🔧 ⛺ ➕ 🏕 🖥 E 📶 P 🛢 ✕ 🏇 🏨 🛢 ◎ 🛢 ✂ 🎣

Leisure facilities: 🎣 🥏 ⛰
Follow road through Torridon Village for 9 mls to Diabaig. Follow road down through village towards the harbour. Take untarred road on left. Caravan first on right.

Key to symbols is on back flap

VAT is shown at 17.5%: changes in this rate may affect prices.   25

DINGWALL, Ross-shire, Map Ref. 4A8

Camping & Caravanning Club Site, Jubilee Park, Dingwall, Ross-shire, IV15 9QZ
☎ *(Dingwall) 01349 862236*
Booking Enquiries: The Camping & Caravanning Club, Greenfields House, Westwood Way, Coventry, CV4 8JH
☎ *(Coventry) 01203 694995 (out of season) Fax: 01203 694886 (out of season)*
4 acres, grassy, stony, level, Mar-Oct, prior booking in peak periods, latest time of arrival 2100. Extra charge for electricity.

🛉 ⚡ ⊙ 🗑 ✦ 🅰 🉐 E 🔣 P ↺ 🐴 ⚬ 🍴 ☎ 💷 D

110 tourers £6.62-7.41 or 110 motors £6.62-7.41 or 110 tents £6.62-7.41.
Total Touring Pitches 110.
From Kessock Bridge on A9, take second left (A835) at Tore roundabout.
Turn right down Hill Street, right in to High Street, left over railway bridge and then first left.

DORNOCH, Sutherland, Map Ref. 4B6

Dornoch Links Caravan & Camping Site, Dornoch, Sutherland, IV25 3LX
☎ *(Dornoch) 01862 810423*
Booking Enquiries: Mr William MacRae, 19 Ross Street, Golspie, Sutherland, KW10 6SA
☎ *(Golspie) 01408 633178*
25 acres, mixed, Apr-Oct, prior booking in peak periods, latest time of arrival 2200. Extra charge for electricity, awnings.

🛉 ⚡ ⊙ 🗑 ✦ 🅰 🉐 🖵 E 🔣 P ↺ ✕ 🐴 ♿ 🏛 ⚠ ⛽ ⚬ 🍴 ☎

100 tourers £6.00-7.00 or 100 motors £6.00-7.00 or 100 tents £5.00-5.50.
Total Touring Pitches 100.
2 Holiday Caravans to let, sleep 4-8 £95.00-180.00, total sleeping capacity 10, min. let 1 night.

🛉 ⚡ 🖵 E 🔣 P ↺ ✕ 🐴 ♿ 🏛 ⚠ ✂ 🗑 ⚱ † D

Leisure facilities: ⚫ ▶ 🏌 ⚓ ∪
From Tain take A9 N for 6 mls. Turn right off A9 on to A949, E for 2 mls.
Entrance via River Street.

Pitgrudy Caravan Park, Dornoch, IV25 3HY
☎ *01862 821253 Fax: 01862 821382*
Booking Enquiries: GNR Sutherland Caravan Sales, Edderton, Ross-shire, IV19 1JY
☎ *(Dornoch) 01862 821253 Fax: 01862 821382*
7 acres, grassy, hard-standing, sloping, May-Sep, prior booking in peak periods, latest time of arrival 2000. Extra charge for electricity, awnings, showers.

🛉 ⚡ ⊙ 🗑 ✦ 🅰 🉐 E 🔣 P 💰 ↺ ✕ 🐴 ⚠ ⚬ 🍴 ☎ SP

30 tourers £7.00-7.50 and 10 motors £7.00-7.50. Total Touring Pitches 40. No tents.
8 Holiday Caravans to let, sleep 2-5 £125.00-250.00, total sleeping capacity 40, min.let 3 nights.

🛉 ⚡ ⊙ 🖵 E 🔣 P 💰 ↺ ✕ 🐴 ⚠ ✂ 🗑 ⚱

Leisure facilities: ✪ ▶ 🏌 ∪
From Dornoch take B9168 N at war memorial. Site approx.³/₄ ml on right.

Important: Prices stated are estimates and may be subject to amendments

DORNOCH, Sutherland, Map Ref. 4B6

Seaview Farm Caravan Park, Hilton, Dornoch, Sutherland
☎ *(Dornoch) 01862 810294*
Booking Enquiries: Mr & Mrs T R Preston
3¹/₂ acres, grassy, sheltered, May-Sep, prior booking in peak periods, latest time of arrival 2100, restricted to Tents Camping Club. Extra charge for electricity.

🦽 ☉ 🗑 🛁 🛋 🎮 wc 🅿 🛍 ✕ 🛒 ⓘ 🎪 🐶 🎯

15 tourers £5.50 or 15 motors £5.50 or 10 tents £5.50. Total Touring Pitches 25.
Turn left at Tourist Office (in square). Site is 1¹/₂ mls on Embo road.
Site entrance on right, opposite telephone kiosk.

Dornoch Caravan Park
Booking Enquiries: Mrs L Dalton, Morven, Schoolhill, Dornoch, Sutherland, IV25 3PF
☎ *(Dornoch) 01862 810412*
Holiday Caravan to let, sleeps 6 £160.00-200.00, min.let 2 nights, Apr-Oct.

🦽 📶 ☉ 🛁 🖳 E wc 🅿 ⏻ ✕ 🛒 🗻 🗄 🧽 🗓 ♨

Leisure facilities: 🔍 ⊕
Approach Dornoch from A9. Drive through town to square, turn right, signposted.
Contact site office for caravan position and keys.

The Links
Booking Enquiries: Mrs D J W Dunbar, Ben Avon Caravans, Station Road, Lairg, Sutherland
☎ *(Lairg) 01549 402428*
2 Holiday Caravans to let, sleep 6 £80.00-180.00, total sleeping capacity 12, min. let 1 night, Apr-Oct.

🦽 📶 🖳 E wc 🅿 ⏻ ✕ 🛒 🍴 🗻 🗄 🧽 🗓 ♨ Ⓣ

Leisure facilities: 🔍
From Inverness take A9 for approx. 50 mls. Turn right at Evelix for Dornoch.

DRUMMORE, Wigtownshire, Map Ref. 1G11

Kilstay Caravan Site
Booking Enquiries: Peter M Irving, Kilstay Caravan Site, Cruachan, Kilstay, Drummore, Stranraer, Wigtownshire, DG9 9QT
☎ *(Drummore) 01776 840249*
3 Holiday Caravans to let, sleep 6 £95.00-120.00, total sleeping capacity 18, min. let weekend, Apr-Oct.

🦽 📶 🚰 E wc 🅿 🛍 ✕ 🛒 🍴 🧽 🗓 ♨

From Stranraer take A716 to Drummore. Park is 1 ml from Drummore.

VAT is shown at 17.5%: changes in this rate may affect prices.

DRUMNADROCHIT, Inverness-shire, Map Ref. 4A9

Å 25

Borlum Farm Caravan and Camping Park, Borlum Farm, Drumnadrochit, Inverness-shire, IV3 6XN

☎ *(Glenurquhart) 01456 450220 Fax: 01456 450358*
2 acres, mixed, 15 Mar-Oct, latest time of arrival 2230, overnight holding area. Extra charge for electricity, awnings, showers.

🔥 🐾 ☉ 🗑 ⚡ 🍴 E 🅦 🅿 🛒 ☾ ✕ 🐕 🛆 🔌 🍴 ⊞ 🆂🅿

10 tourers £6.00-7.00 or 10 motors £6.00-7.00 or 15 tents £5.00-5.50.
Total Touring Pitches 25.

Leisure facilities: ⤴ ∪ 🛆 ✦ ⚘

Near Lewiston and Drumnadrochit by Loch Ness on A82 from Inverness-Fort Augustus.

DUNBAR, East Lothian, Map Ref. 2E4

Å 80

Camping & Caravanning Club Site, Barns Ness, Dunbar, East Lothian, EH42 1QP

☎ *(Dunbar) 01368 863536*
Booking Enquiries: The Camping and Caravanning Club, Greenfields House, Westwood Way, Coventry, CV4 8JH
☎ *(Coventry) 01203 694995 (out of season) Fax: 01203 694886 (out of season)*
10 acres, grassy, sandy, level, Mar-Oct, prior booking in peak periods, latest time of arrival 2100, overnight holding area. Extra charge for electricity.

🔥 🐾 ☉ 🗑 ⚡ 🍴 E 🅦 🅿 ☾ ✕ 🐕 🛆 🍴 ⊞

80 tourers £5.72-6.40 or 80 motors £5.72-6.40 or 80 tents £5.72-6.40.
Total Touring Pitches 80.

Leisure facilities: ⤴ ⚘ 🛆

Look for signpost East Barns 20 mls N of Berwick on Tweed on A1 road.
Turn at junction, signposted to site.

DUNKELD, Perthshire, Map Ref. 2B1

Å 278

Erigmore House Holiday Park, Birnam, Dunkeld, Perthshire, PH8 9XX

☎ *(Dunkeld) 01350 727236*
Booking Enquiries: Parkdean Holidays Ltd, Cragside House, 42a Heaton Road, Newcastle upon Tyne, Tyne & Wear
☎ *0191 224 0500 Fax: 0191 224 0490*
27 acres, grassy, mid Mar-Oct, prior booking in peak periods, latest time of arrival 2200, overnight holding area. Extra charge for electricity, awnings.

🔥 🐾 🚐 ☉ 🗑 ⚡ 🛒 🍴 🖵 🅦 🅿 🛒 ☾ ✕ 🐕 🏵 🔺 ▲ 🍷 🆁 🍽 🚿 🛆 🎵 🍴 🛒 ⊞ 🅣 🆂🅿

52 tourers £11.00-15.00 or 52 motors £11.00-15.00 or 52 tents £6.00-9.00.
Total Touring Pitches 52.
70 Holiday Caravans to let, sleep 4-8 £105.00-390.00, total sleeping capacity 420, min. let weekend.

🔥 🐾 ☉ 🛒 🖵 E 🅦 🅿 ☾ 🐕 🏵 ▲ 🖵 ✍ 🍽 🚿 ⊞ 🅣

Leisure facilities: 🎱 🏊 🏌 ⚓ 🎣 ● ► ⤴ ∪

From Perth take A9 N for 11 mls. Turn right to Birnam. 200 yds further on turn right past the Shell garage to Erigmore.

DUNOON, Argyll, Map Ref. 1G5

Stratheck Caravan Park
Loch Eck, by Dunoon, Argyll PA23 8SG
Telephone: (01369) 840472   Fax: (01369) 840 472
Gateway to the Western Highlands. Luxury caravans set amidst
magnificent scenery for hire, £140-£250 per week. Excellent facilities
including country club, games room, laundry, shop. Fishing, boating,
golfing, hiking available. Tourers, tents, motorhomes welcome.
Hook-ups. Half price Clyde ferry tickets available.
Contact: F.J. Brassington, Loch Eck, Dunoon, Argyll PA23 8SG

Stratheck International Caravan Park, Inverchapel, Loch Eck, by Dunoon, Argyll, PA23 8SG
☎ *(Kilmun)* 0136984 472/01369 840472
13 acres, grassy, hard-standing, level, Apr-Oct, latest time of arrival 2200,
overnight holding area. Extra charge for electricity, awnings.

20 tourers £6.00-8.00 or 20 motors £6.00-8.00 or 20 tents £5.00-8.00.
Total Touring Pitches 20.
4 Holiday Caravans to let, sleep 6 £140.00-245.00, total sleeping capacity 24,
min.let 3 nights.

Leisure facilities: ● ☻ ⴹ ♪ ⌇ ∪ ◬
From Dunoon take the A815. Travel for 7 mls. Site on left of road ¹/₂ ml beyond
Younger Botanic Garden. Signposted.

ECCLEFECHAN, Dumfriesshire, Map Ref. 2C9

Cressfield Caravan Park, Ecclefechan, Dumfriesshire, DG11 3RD
☎ *(Ecclefechan)* 01576 300702
30 acres, grassy, hard-standing, level, Jan-Dec, latest time of arrival 2200,
overnight holding area. Extra charge for electricity, awnings.

67 tourers £6.00-7.50 or 67 motors £6.00-7.50 or 67 tents £6.00.
Total Touring Pitches 67.
Holiday Caravan to let, sleeps 6 £80.00-180.00, min. let 2 nights.

Leisure facilities: ☻
10 mls N of Gretna.¹/₄ ml from A/M74 at Ecclefechan. S of village.

Hoddom Castle Caravan Park, Hoddom, Lockerbie, Dumfriesshire, DG11 1AS
☎ *(Ecclefechan)* 01576 300251
28 acres, mixed, Easter-Oct, prior booking in peak periods, latest time of arrival 2130,
overnight holding area. Extra charge for electricity, awnings.

150 tourers £6.50-10.00 or 150 motors £6.50-10.00 or 150 tents £6.50-10.00.
Total Touring Pitches 150.
Leisure facilities: ● ☻ ⌇ ⴹ ♪
Turn off A74 at Ecclefechan. At church to B725, W to Dalton, Entrance 2¹/₂ mls
W of Ecclefechan.

Key to symbols
is on back flap

VAT is shown at 17.5%: changes in this rate may affect prices.

EDINBURGH, Map Ref. 2D5

Little France Caravan Park, 219 Old Dalkeith Road, Edinburgh, EH16 4SU
☎ *0131 666 2326*
10 acres, grassy, stony, level, Apr-Oct, prior booking in peak periods, latest time of arrival 2200. Extra charge for electricity, awnings.

287

🔧♠⊙⬛✂🛢️📶🅿🐾🕁✗🍴🔔♨🛒🔔D

287 tourers £8.00-9.00 or 287 motors £8.00-9.00 or 287 tents £8.00-9.00.
Total Touring Pitches 287.
Situated on A7 road from Edinburgh to Newcastle.

Mortonhall Caravan Park, Edinburgh

Country estate situated just 15 mins. from city centre and 5 mins. from the bypass. Parkland estate hosts premier graded park. Luxury holiday homes, touring and tenting pitches. Excellent amenities - modern toilet and shower block, restaurant and bar, shop, games room, TV room and laundry. An ideal base to see Edinburgh and Southern Scotland. Free colour brochure and tariff.

DEPT STB C&C

Mortonhall Caravan Park
Frogston Road East, Edinburgh EH16 6TJ

Tel: 0131-664 1533, Fax: 0131-664 5387
Prices: Min £8.00, Max £11.00

Mortonhall Caravan Park, 38 Mortonhall Gate, Frogston Rd East, Edinburgh, EH16 6TJ
☎ *0131 664 1533 Fax: 0131 664 5387*
22 acres, mixed, Apr-Oct, prior booking in peak periods, latest time of arrival 2100, overnight holding area. Extra charge for electricity, awnings.

268

🔧♠⊙⬛✂🛢️📶⬜E🆆🅿🕁✗🍴♨⚠🔔R♻♨🛒🔔♨🔔❌🎎🛡️T SP

250 tourers £8.00-11.00 or 250 motors £8.00-11.00 or 250 tents £8.00-11.00.
Total Touring Pitches 250.
14 Holiday Caravans to let, sleep 6 £135.00-360.00, total sleeping capacity 84, min. let 3 days.

🔧♠➡⊙⬜E🆆🅿🕁✗🍴♨⚠🔔♻♨♨❌🎎T D

Leisure facilities: ● ⊕ ► ∪ ⟑
From N or S leave city bypass at Straiton junction and follow signs for Mortonhall.
From city take main road S from E or W end of Princes Street.

ELGIN, Moray, Map Ref. 4D8

Riverside Caravan Park, West Road, Elgin, Moray, IV30 3UN
☎ *(Elgin) 01343 542813*
5¹/₂ acres, mixed, Apr-Oct, prior booking in peak periods, latest time of arrival 2400, overnight holding area. Extra charge for electricity.

48

🔧♠➡⊙⬛✂🛢️📶⬜E🆆🅿🐾🕁✗🍴⚠♨🔔♨🔔D

47 tourers £6.00-8.00 or 47 motors £6.00-8.00 or 47 tents £5.50.
Total Touring Pitches 47.
Leisure facilities: ⊕ ► ∫ ∪ ◊ ⟑
On A96 immediately W of Elgin.

ELIE, Fife, Map Ref. 2E3

250

Shell Bay Caravan Site, Abbeyford Caravans, Elie, Fife, KY9
☎ (Elie) 01333 330283
50 acres, grassy, sandy, mid Mar-Oct, prior booking in peak periods, overnight holding area. Extra charge for electricity, awnings.

120 tourers £8.00-10.00 or 120 motors £8.00-10.00 or 120 tents £7.50-9.00.
Total Touring Pitches 120.
3 Holiday Caravans to let, sleep 6 £100.00-200.00, total sleeping capacity 18, min. let weekend.

Leisure facilities: 🎣 🌐
Take M90 N or S, turn off on A911, signposted Glenrothes. Continue on A911 to Leven, follow A921 through Upper Largo. Site before Elie.

EMBO, Sutherland, Map Ref. 4B6

Grannies Heilan Hame Holiday Park

EMBO, DORNOCH
SUTHERLAND IV25 3QP
Tel: (01862) 810383

Thistle Commended accommodation. Indoor swimming pool. Nearby is the world famous Royal Dornoch Golf Course. Nightly entertainment from April 28-Oct 1 (weekends only outside these dates). New for '95 – 2 tennis courts, soft play room and games room – amusements, darts, pool, take-away food, late bars and meals. Launderette and mini-supermarket. Tourers welcome.

Prices: £80-£395 per week.   Quote Ref. STB
Contact Parkdean Holidays
(0191) 2240500. Brochure

Grannies Heilan Hame Holiday Park, Embo, Dornoch, Sutherland, IV25 3QP
☎ (Dornoch) 01862 810383
Booking Enquiries: Parkdean Holidays Ltd, Cragside House, 42a Heaton Road, Newcastle upon Tyne, Tyne & Wear, NE6 1SE
☎ 0191 224 0500 Fax: 0191 224 0490
32 acres, grassy, sandy, level, Jan-Oct, prior booking in peak periods, latest time of arrival 2300, overnight holding area. Extra charge for electricity.

224 tourers £7.00-12.50 or 224 motors £7.00-12.50 or 100 tents £7.00-10.00.
Total Touring Pitches 324.
89 Holiday Caravans to let, sleep 6-8 £100.00-420.00, total sleeping capacity 540, min. let 2 nights.

Leisure facilities:
A9 from Inverness via Kessock Bridge to Dornoch. Then left at Main Square to Embo (3 mls) beside Grannies Heilan Hame park.

Key to symbols is on back flap

VAT is shown at 17.5%: changes in this rate may affect prices.

EVANTON, Ross-shire, Map Ref. 4A8

Black Rock Caravan Site, Evanton, Ross-shire, IV16 9UN
☎ *(Evanton) 01349 830917 Fax: 01349 830321*
4¹/₂ acres, grassy, level, sheltered, Apr-Oct, prior booking in peak periods, latest time of arrival 2200, overnight holding area. Extra charge for electricity, awnings.

🚻 🏞 ☉ 🗟 ⚡ 🖴 🏕 E 🚾 P 🏊 ☯ ✕ 🐕 🎠 🏔 � 🍽 🛒

45 tourers £7.00-10.00 or 45 motors £7.00-10.00 or 10 tents £5.00-8.00.
Total Touring Pitches 55.
6 Holiday Caravans to let, sleep 4-8 £150.00-250.00, total sleeping capacity 38, min. let 2 nights.

🚻 🏞 🚮 ☉ 🖴 🖵 E 🚾 P 🏊 ☯ ✕ 🐕 🎠 🏔 🗄 ⌀ 🗄 🛢 Ⓓ

Leisure facilities: ⊕ ⚲ ♪
A9 N from Inverness for 12 mls, turn left for Evanton B817 proceed for ³/₄ ml.

EYEMOUTH, Berwickshire, Map Ref. 2G5

Northburn Holiday Home Park, Eyemouth, Berwickshire, TD14 5ER
☎ *(Eyemouth) 018907 51050 Fax: 018907 51462*
Booking Enquiries: Mr L Wood
25 acres, mixed, Mar-Nov, prior booking in peak periods, latest time of arrival 2000.
Extra charge for electricity, awnings.

🚻 🏞 🚮 ☉ 🗟 🖴 🏕 🖵 E 🚾 P 🏊 ☯ ✕ 🐕 🎠 🏔 🍴 Ⓡ ♨ ♪ 🍽 🛒 ⊞ SP

40 tourers £6.00-11.00 or 40 motors £6.00-9.50. Total Touring Pitches 40. No tents.
20 Holiday Caravans to let, sleep 4-8 £90.00-295.00, total sleeping capacity 132, min. let 2 nights.

🚻 🏞 🚮 ☉ 🖴 🖵 E 🚾 P 🏊 ☯ ✕ 🐕 🎠 🏔 🗄 ⌀ 🗄 🛢 ⊞ Ⓓ

Leisure facilities: ⚲ ♪ ⚲
From Berwick-on-Tweed, leave A1 at Burnmouth. Well signposted.

FINDHORN, Moray, Map Ref. 4C8

Findhorn Bay Caravan Park, Findhorn, Forres, Moray, IV36 0TY
☎ *(Findhorn) 01309 690203 Fax: 01309 690933*
22 acres, mixed, Apr-Oct, prior booking in peak periods, latest time of arrival 2100.
Extra charge for electricity, awnings.

🚻 🏞 ☉ 🗟 ⚡ 🖴 🏕 E 🚾 P 🏊 ☯ ✕ 🐕 🎠 🏔 Ⓡ ♨ ♨ 🛢 🍽 🛒 ⊞ SP

75 tourers £6.00-7.50 or 75 motors £6.00-7.50 or 50 tents £4.00-4.50.
Total Touring Pitches 75.
16 Holiday Caravans to let, sleep 4-7 £110.00-270.00, total sleeping capacity 86, min.,let 2 days.

🚻 🏞 🚮 ☉ 🖴 🖵 E 🚾 P ☯ ✕ 🎠 🏔 🗄 ⌀ 🗄 🛢 ⊞

Leisure facilities: ▶ ♪ ∪ ⛰ ⚵ ⚓
From A96 in Forres take B9011 to Kinloss, then turn left for Findhorn.
Site entrance 2 mls on right.

FINDHORN, Moray, Map Ref. 4C8

Findhorn Sands Caravan Park, Findhorn, Forres, Moray, IV36 0YZ
☎ (Findhorn) 01309 630324
30 acres, grassy, level, Apr-Oct, prior booking in peak periods, latest time of arrival 1900.
Extra charge for electricity, awnings.

30 tourers £8.00-9.00 and 10 motors £8.00-9.00 and 10 tents £5.00-6.00.
Total Touring Pitches 50.

Leisure facilities: 🦆 🦆 🛶 🦆
Take B9011 from Forres, turn left at Kinloss to Findhorn, through Findhorn,
turn right before Culbin Sands Hotel.

FINTRY, Stirlingshire, Map Ref. 2A4

BALGAIR CASTLE

Overglinns, Fintry, Stirlingshire G63 0LP
Telephone: 01360 860283
★ *Winner of Calor Award*
'Most Improved Park in Scotland 1993' ★
★ *Winner of Antartex Award*
'Best Camping & Caravan Park' ★

BALGAIR CASTLE is situated on the banks of the River Endrick.
Nestling in the valley between Campsie and Fintry hills, the
ancient stronghold of Culreuch (Fintry Village) is tranquil yet
close to Glasgow, Loch Lomond, the Trossachs and Stirling.
Hillwalking, pony-trekking, fishing and golf nearby. Holiday
homes for hire. Private Club with regular entertainment for
exclusive use of park visitors. Food and laundry available.
Children's Play Area and Shop.

HOLIDAY HOMES £100-£280 per week.
TOURERS from £7.50 per night. Electric hook-ups available.

Contact Mrs M Lamb
Fintry 01360 860283 Fax: 01360 860300

Balgair Castle Caravan Park, Overglinns, Fintry, Stirlingshire, G63 0LP
☎ (Fintry) 01360 860283 Fax: 01360 860300
35 acres, grassy, Mar-Oct (tourers), Mar-Nov (homes), prior booking in peak periods,
latest time of arrival 2200, overnight holding area. Extra charge for electricity, awnings.

63 tourers £7.75-8.75 or 10 motors £6.65-7.75 or 6 tents £5.00-7.75.
Total Touring Pitches 63.
3 Holiday Caravans to let, sleep 6 £160.00-240.00, total sleeping capacity 18,
min. let weekend.

Leisure facilities: ♨ 🎯 🦆 ↻
B822 Fintry-Kippen, 1½ mls N of Fintry.

Key to symbols
is on back flap

VAT is shown at 17.5%: changes in this rate may affect prices.

FORFAR, Angus, Map Ref. 2D1

Lochside Caravan Park, Forfar Country Park, Forfar, Angus, DD8
☎ *(Forfar) 01307 464201*
Booking Enquiries: Lochside Leisure Centre, Forfar Country Park, Forfar, Angus, DD8
☎ *(Forfar) 01307 464201*
4.9 acres, grassy, level, Apr-early Oct, prior booking in peak periods,
latest time of arrival 2100. Extra charge for electricity.

🔌 🔥 ☉ 🗑 ✄ 🚿 E 🚾 🅿 🧺 ✕ 🐴 ⚠ 🍽 Ⓡ 🧺 🛢 🤿 🎣 Ⓓ

74 tourers £7.70-8.85 or 74 motors £7.70-8.85 or 74 tents £3.45-4.60.
Total Touring Pitches 74.

Leisure facilities: 🎱 ⛳

¹/₂ ml NW of Forfar off A90 on E shore of Forfar Loch, adjacant to Lochside Leisure Centre.

FORTROSE, Ross-shire, Map Ref. 4B8

Booking Enquiries: Mrs L J Grant, Fasgadh, Ness Road, Fortrose, Ross-shire
☎ *(Fortrose) 01381 620367*
Holiday Caravan to let, sleeps 6 £95.00-150.00, min.let weekend, Easter-Sep.

🔌 🔥 ☉ 🛒 🖥 E 🚾 🅿 🧺 ✕ 🐴 🏠 🧽 🖲 🛢 🎿 ✗

From Fortrose to Rosemarkie Ness Road is on right at church/police station.
First house on left side of Ness Road.

QUALITY
YOU WANT IT. WE OFFER IT.

Important: Prices stated are estimates and may be subject to amendments

FORT WILLIAM, Inverness-shire, Map Ref. 3G12

GLEN NEVIS CARAVAN AND CAMPING PARK
Glen Nevis, Fort William, Inverness-shire PH33 6SX
Tel: 01397 702191   Fax: 01397 703904

Beautifully situated in one of Scotland's most famous glens yet only 2¹/₂ miles from the historic town of Fort William. The park has separate areas for tourers and tents and offers modern clean and well-equipped facilities. Excellent tour centre for the Western Highlands.

GLEN NEVIS HOLIDAY CARAVANS

Quality caravans for holiday let in a magnificent setting only 2¹/₂ miles from the historic town of Fort William. Enjoy peaceful surroundings with lots to see and do nearby. Caravans are well equipped and have full facilities. Phone/write for colour brochure.

GLEN NEVIS HOLIDAY CARAVANS
Glen Nevis, Fort William, Inverness-shire PH33 6SX
Tel: 01397 702191 Fax: 01397 703904

280

Glen Nevis Caravan & Camping Park, Glen Nevis, Fort William, Inverness-shire, PH33 6SX
☎ (Fort William) 01397 702191 Fax: 01397 703904
23 acres, mixed, mid Mar-mid Oct, prior booking in peak periods, latest time of arrival 2200. Extra charge for electricity, awnings, showers.

250 tourers £6.00-8.50 or 250 motors £5.70-8.20 or 130 tents £5.30-8.20. Total Touring Pitches 380.
29 Holiday Caravans to let, sleep 2-6 £155.00-315.00, total sleeping capacity 154, min. let 3 nights.

Leisure facilities: ▶ ∪ ⚐
From A82 at r/about N of Fort William, turn E signed Glen Nevis. Park 2.5 mls on right, signposted Glen Nevis Holiday Caravans.

TELEPHONE DIALLING CODES

On 16 April 1995 all UK area codes starting **0** will start **01**.

From August 1994 until 16 April 1995, the new codes will be run in parallel with the old ones.
If you experience difficulty in connecting a call, please call Directory Enquiries – **192** – for advice. Please note: A charge will be made for this service when using a private phone.

VAT is shown at 17.5%: changes in this rate may affect prices.

FORT WILLIAM, Inverness-shire, Map Ref. 3G12

190

Linnhe Caravan Park Ltd, Corpach, Fort William, Inverness-shire, PH33 7NL
☎ *(Corpach) 01397 772376 Fax: 01397 772007*
13¹/₂ acres, hard-standing, sheltered, mid Dec-Oct, prior booking in peak periods.
Extra charge for electricity, awnings.

81 tourers £7.75-9.25 or 81 motors £7.75-9.25. Total Touring Pitches 86. No tents.
83 Holiday Caravans to let, sleep 1-8 £120.00-358.00, total sleeping capacity 484, min. let 2 nights.

On A830, 1¹/₂ mls W of Corpach village.

120

Lochy Caravan & Camping Park, Camaghael, Fort William, Inverness-shire, PH33 7NF
☎ *(Fort William) 01397 703446 Fax: 01397 706172*
6 acres, grassy, sheltered, Apr-Oct, latest time of arrival 2100.
Extra charge for electricity, awnings.

40 tourers £7.10-9.60 and 40 motors £6.90-9.30 and 40 tents £6.90-9.30.
Total Touring Pitches 120.
13 Holiday Caravans to let, sleep 4-6 £200.00-340.00, total sleeping capacity 78, min.let 3 nights.

Leisure facilities: ⚓
2 mls N of Fort William turn off A82 on to A830 for 700 yds.
Turn right at High school. Signposted at A82/A830 junction.

GAIRLOCH, Ross-shire, Map Ref. 3F7

50

Gairloch Holiday Park, Strath, Gairloch, Ross-shire
☎ *(Gairloch) 01445 2373*
Booking Enquiries: Mrs Joan Forbes, 70 St Andrews Drive, Bridge of Weir, Renfrewshire, PA11 3HY
☎ *(Bridge of Weir) 01505 614343*
6 acres, grassy, hard-standing, level, Apr-Oct, latest time of arrival 2100.
Extra charge for electricity, awnings.

25 tourers £5.00-8.00 and 10 motors £5.00-7.00 and 15 tents £4.50-6.00.
Total Touring Pitches 50.
Holiday Caravan to let, sleeps 4-6 £140.00-160.00.

Leisure facilities: 🔍 ▶ 🎣
From A832 take B8021 for ¹/₄ ml, turn right at Millcroft Hotel.

Important: Prices stated are estimates and may be subject to amendments

GAIRLOCH, Ross-shire, Map Ref. 3F7

Sands Holiday Centre, Gairloch, Ross-shire, IV21 2DL
☎ *(Gairloch) 01445 712152*
50 acres, mixed, Apr-Oct, prior booking in peak periods, latest time of arrival 2230.
Extra charge for electricity, awnings.

120 tourers from £6.50 and 40 motors from £6.50 and 200 tents from £6.50.
Total Touring Pitches 360.
5 Holiday Caravans to let, sleep 6 from £195.00, total sleeping capacity 30,
min. let 2 nights.

Leisure facilities:
At Gairloch turn on to B8021 (Melvaig). Site 3 mls on, beside sandy beach.

BY GARDENSTOWN, Banffshire, Map Ref. 4G7

Booking Enquiries: Mrs Smith, Bankhead Croft, Gamrie, Banffshire, AB45 3HN
☎ *(Gardenstown) 01261 851584*
Holiday Caravan to let, sleeps 6 £50.00-110.00, min. let 1 night, Jan-Dec.

Leisure facilities:
From Banff take A98 to Fraserburgh for 6 mls. Turn left at Gardenstown sign.
Caravan is 2 mls on at Bankhead Croft.

GARTOCHARN, by Balloch, Dunbartonshire, Map Ref. 1H4

Lagganbeg Caravan Park, Gartocharn, by Balloch, Dunbartonshire, G83 8NQ
☎ *(Gartocharn) 01389 830281*
3¼ acres, mixed, Mar-Jan, prior booking in peak periods, latest time of arrival 2200.
Extra charge for electricity, awnings.

12 tourers £7.00-8.00 or 12 motors £7.00-8.00 or 30 tents £5.00.
Total Touring Pitches 12.
Leisure facilities:
A811 from Balloch to Gartocharn. Turn left at caravan sign.

GATEHOUSE-OF-FLEET, Kirkcudbrightshire, Map Ref. 2A10

Auchenlarie Holiday Farm, Gatehouse of Fleet, Kirkcudbrightshire, DG7 2EX
☎ *(Mossyard) 01557 840251 Fax: 01557 840252*
20 acres, grassy, sandy, hard-standing, Mar-Oct, latest time of arrival 0100,
overnight holding area. Extra charge for electricity, awnings, showers.

127 tourers £4.00-8.00 or 127 motors £4.00-8.00 or 127 tents £4.00-8.00.
Total Touring Pitches 127.
37 Holiday Caravans to let, sleep 4-6 £99.00-255.00, total sleeping capacity 222,
min. let weekend.

Leisure facilities:
A75 4 mls W of Gatehouse-of-Fleet.

Key to symbols
is on back flap

VAT is shown at 17.5%: changes in this rate may affect prices.

GATEHOUSE OF FLEET, Kirkcudbrightshire, Map Ref. 2A10

Mossyard Caravan Site, Gatehouse of Fleet, Kirkcudbrightshire, DG7 2ET
☎ *(Mossyard) 01557 840226*
6 acres, grassy, sandy, Apr-Oct, prior booking in peak periods.
Extra charge for electricity, awnings, showers.

10 tourers £5.00-6.00 and 10 motors £5.00 and 10 tents £4.00-6.00.
Total Touring Pitches 30.
From Gatehouse-of-Fleet take A75 W for 4½ mls, turn left at Mossyard sign,
100 yds past white cottage on left.

GLASGOW, Map Ref. 1H5

Craigendmuir Park, Campsie View, Stepps, Glasgow, G33 6AF
☎ *0141 779 4159/2973 Fax: 0141 779 4057*
2½ acres, mixed, Jan-Dec, prior booking in peak periods, latest time of arrival 2100,
overnight holding area. Extra charge for electricity.

20 tourers from £5.50 or 20 motors from £5.50 or 10 tents from £5.50.
Total Touring Pitches 20.
12 Holiday Caravans to let, sleep 4 £95.00-160.00, total sleeping capacity 48.

From S & W exit junction 11 on M8 and follow A80 Cumbernauld/Stirling.
From N on A80 to Stepps.

GLENCOE, Argyll, Map Ref. 1F1

Invercoe Caravans, Invercoe, Glencoe, Argyll
☎ *(Ballachulish) 018552 210*
5 acres, grassy, hard-standing, level, Apr-Oct. Extra charge for electricity, awnings.

35 tourers £7.00-8.00 and 10 motors £7.00-8.00 and 10 tents £7.00-8.00.
Total Touring Pitches 55.
5 Holiday Caravans to let, sleep 4 £140.00-250.00, total sleeping capacity 20.

On B863 ¼ ml from Glencoe crossroads.

TELEPHONE DIALLING CODES

On 16 April 1995 all UK area codes starting **0** will start **01**.

From August 1994 until 16 April 1995, the new codes will be run in parallel with the old ones.
If you experience difficulty in connecting a call, please call Directory Enquiries – **192** – for advice. Please note: A charge will be made for this service when using a private phone.

GLENDARUEL, Argyll, Map Ref. 1F4

Glendaruel Caravan Park
Glendaruel, Argyll PA22 3AB   Tel: (01369) 820267

Unwind and relax in the tranquil atmosphere of this beautiful small park, personally run by the owners Quin and Anne Craig since 1976. Discover this area of outstanding natural beauty, quiet roads, hidden sandy beaches. Great walking, sea-trout and salmon fishing, bird-watching. Kyles of Bute 5 miles. Bicycles for hire. Excellent eating out. *Reduced Clyde Ferry fares and various other discounts.*
Thistle Award-winning Caravans for hire with colour TV.
NEW ALL-WEATHER PITCHES FOR TOURERS
For colour brochure and further information please telephone 01369 820267
AA ▶ ▶ ▶   RAC Caravan Club Approved Member BH, HPA & NCC

Glendaruel Caravan Park, Glendaruel, Argyll, PA22 3AB
☎ *(Glendaruel)* 01369 820267 Fax: 01369 820267
3 acres, mixed, Apr-Oct, prior booking in peak periods, latest time of arrival 2200, overnight holding area. Extra charge for electricity, awnings.

25 tourers from £7.50 or 25 motors from £7.50 or 25 tents from £7.50.
Total Touring Pitches 25.
5 Holiday Caravans to let, sleep 6 £125.00-310.00, total sleeping capacity 30, min. let 2 days.

Leisure facilities: ● ✪ ▶ ♪ ◢ ∪ ✓ ☒ ▲ ➤ ⚓
From Strachur (Loch Fyne) take A886 S for 13 mls, turn right at sign. Alternative route – Ferry to Dunoon then on B836 which joins A886 approx. 4 mls S of Park.

GLEN ESK, by Edzell, Angus, Map Ref. 4F12

GLENESK CARAVAN PARK
Edzell, Angus DD9 7YP   Tel: (01356) 648565

The Park is situated in a peaceful woodland setting surrounding a small lake. All amenities. Games room. TV, reception, lounge, tuck shop, ideal centre for walking, touring, fishing, golf, grass camping area. Limited static hire.

RAC L AA ★ ★ ★   *Open April-October*

Glenesk Caravan Park, Glen Esk, by Edzell, Angus, DD9 7YP
☎ *(Edzell)* 01356 648565
8 acres, mixed, Apr-Oct, prior booking in peak periods, latest time of arrival 2100, overnight holding area. Extra charge for electricity.

45 tourers £6.00-7.00 or 45 motors £6.00-7.00 or 15 tents £5.00-6.00.
Total Touring Pitches 45.
3 Holiday Caravans to let, sleep 4-6 £182.00-210.00, total sleeping capacity 16, min.let 3 days.

Leisure facilities: ● ✪ ♪ ∪
A94 turn off at Edzell junction B966, out of Edzell, site signposted from Gannochy Bridge.

Key to symbols
is on back flap

GLENISLA, Angus, Map Ref. 2C1

Small award-winning touring park in unspoilt rural setting,
four miles north of Alyth.
An ideal base for touring, with many activities and much
of historic interest nearby.
Open from mid-March to mid-October.
Caravans, motorvans and tents welcome.

NETHER CRAIG CARAVAN PARK

Nether Craig, Alyth, Blairgowrie, Perthshire PH11 8HN Telephone: (01575) 560204 Fax: (01575) 560315

Nether Craig Caravan Park, by Alyth, Blairgowrie, Perthshire, PH11 8HN
☎ *(Lintrathen) 01575 560204 Fax: 01575 560315*
4½ acres, grassy, hard-standing, level, sheltered, mid Mar-mid Oct,

prior booking in peak periods, latest time of arrival 2100, overnight holding area.
Extra charge for electricity.

40 tourers £7.00-9.00 or 40 motors £7.00-9.00 or 40 tents £7.00-9.00.
Total Touring Pitches 40.

Leisure facilities: ✪
South of Alyth, join B954 signposted Glenisla. After 4 mls turn right onto
unclassified road signposted Nether Craig Caravan Park. Site ½ ml on left.

GLENLUCE, Wigtownshire, Map Ref. 1G10

Whitecairn Farm Caravan Park, Whitecairn, Glenluce, Wigtownshire, DG8 0NZ
☎ *(Glenluce) 01581 300267 Fax: 01581 300267*
6 acres, grassy, hard-standing, level, Mar-Oct, prior booking in peak periods,
latest time of arrival 2200. Extra charge for electricity, awnings.

10 tourers £6.50-7.50 or 10 motors £6.50-7.50 or 10 tents £6.50-7.50.
Total Touring Pitches 10.
16 Holiday Caravans to let, sleep 2-6 £120.00-275.00, total sleeping capacity 96,
min. let 2 nights.

Leisure facilities: ✪ ▶ ✦ ✦ ∪
1½ mls north of Glenluce village.

GORTHLECK, Inverness-shire, Map Ref. 4A10

Booking Enquiries: Miss D Fraser, Trinloist, Gorthleck, Inverness-shire
☎ *(Glenurquhart) 01456 486397*
Holiday Caravan to let, sleeps 4-6 £80.00-120.00, min. let 1 night, Jan-Dec.

From A9 take B851 to Gorthleck

GRANTOWN-ON-SPEY, Moray, Map Ref. 4C9

GRANTOWN-ON-SPEY CARAVAN PARK

Seafield Avenue, Grantown-on-Spey, Moray PH26 3JQ
Tel: (01479) 872474   Fax: (01479) 873696

Situated in the heart of the Highlands where time stands still. Take the Malt Whisky Trail, fish the Spey and golf in beautiful surroundings. A bird watcher's Mecca and paradise for dogs!

Graded 'Excellent', we offer a friendly welcome, peace and tranquillity. Open 31 March until 30 September.

Grantown-on-Spey Caravan Park, Seafield Avenue, Grantown-on-Spey, Moray, PH26 3JQ
☎ *(Grantown-on-Spey) 01479 872474 Fax: 01479 873696*
23 acres, mixed, Apr-Sep, prior booking in peak periods, latest time of arrival 2200, overnight holding area. Extra charge for electricity, awnings.

154

50 tourers from £7.00 and 50 motors from £7.00 and 50 tents from £5.50.
Total Touring Pitches 150.
6 Holiday Caravans to let, sleep 2-5 £135.00-245.00, total sleeping capacity 24, min. let weekend.

Leisure facilities:
Park ½ ml from town centre. Turn N by Bank of Scotland.

GREENLAW, Berwickshire, Map Ref. 2F6

Greenlaw Caravan Park, Greenlaw, Berwickshire, TD10 6XX
☎ *(Greenlaw) 01361 810341*
5¼ acres, grassy, hard-standing, level, Mar-Nov, latest time of arrival 2200, overnight holding area. Extra charge for electricity.

65

10 tourers £7.00 or 10 motors £6.00 or 10 tents £7.00. Total Touring Pitches 10.
At crossroads of A697 and A6105 centre of Greenlaw village, 37 mls S of Edinburgh.

HADDINGTON, East Lothian, Map Ref. 2E5

The Monks' Muir

Haddington, East Lothian EH41 3SB
Telephone: (01620) 860340 Fax: (01620) 860340
Glorious, very friendly, gently wooded, informal, green, super views, continental ambience. In the heart of East Lothian yet only 25 minutes from Edinburgh. Appointed by everyone, every possible facility, super shop. Described as 'AN UNEXPECTED GEM'.
Tents, Tourers, Campervans or 'THISTLE AWARD' hire caravans, very carefully prepared and thoughtfully presented.

The Monks' Muir, Haddington, East Lothian
☎ *(East Linton) 01620 860340 Fax: 01620 860340*
7 acres, mixed, Jan-Dec, prior booking in peak periods, latest time of arrival 2400.
Extra charge for electricity, awnings.

92

70 tourers £9.00 or 70 motors £9.00 or 70 tents £8.00. Total Touring Pitches 70.
6 Holiday Caravans to let, sleep 6-8 £90.00-295.00, total sleeping capacity 40, min. let nightly.

Leisure facilities:
Directly on the A1, midway between Haddington and East Linton.

Key to symbols
is on back flap

INVERARAY, Argyll, Map Ref. 1F3

Argyll Caravan Park
Inveraray, Argyll PA32 8XT   Tel: (01499) 302285
Attractively situated on shores of Loch Fyne, 2¹/₂ miles south of Inveraray on A83. All normal amenities including shop, lounge bar (children welcome), recreation hall, launderette. Tourer stances with electricity and water and TV points. Luxury caravans with lochside position, 3-bedroom £200-£300 per week. Open 1st April-31st October.
Contact: The Manager (01499) 302285.

Argyll Caravan Park, Inveraray, Argyll, PA32
☎ *(Inveraray) 01499 302285*
50 acres, mixed, Apr-Oct, prior booking in peak periods, overnight holding area. Extra charge for electricity, awnings.

270

🛠 📶 ⏚ ⊙ 🔞 ∥ 🛢 🍺 🖵 E 🆆 P 🧺 ↻ ✕ 🐎 🐕 ⚠ 🍽 Ⓡ 🎿 ♿ 🔥 🔫 🎪

60 tourers £7.50-9.00 or 60 motors £7.50-9.00 or 20 tents £6.00-7.50.
Total Touring Pitches 80.
11 Holiday Caravans to let, sleep 6 £200.00-300.00, total sleeping capacity 66, min. let weekend.

🛠 📶 ⏚ 🖵 E 🆆 P ↻ ✕ 🐎 ⚠ ∅ 🔥 🔨 Ⓓ

Leisure facilities: ◔ ✪ ∪
From Glasgow A82 to Tarbet then A83 to Inveraray. Park is 2 mls S of Inveraray.

INVERBEG, by Luss, Dunbartonshire, Map Ref. 1G4

LOCH LOMOND

INVERBEG HOLIDAY PARK

Inverbeg, by Luss, Dunbartonshire G83 8PD
Telephone: (01436) 860267

ON LOCH LOMOND, with private beach, good boat launching and excellent sea-trout fishing from the shore. In a position of outstanding beauty, and kept very clean and tidy. Shop and launderette on the park.

Activity play area and games room. Restaurant 200 yards away. Boat trips and other activities nearby.

HOLIDAY CARAVANS for hire with colour TV. Fully serviced, shower, wc, H&C, full-size cooker and fridge, minimum of two bedrooms, equipped to a very high standard, two and three bedroom extra wide models (12') available.

| ✓ | ✓ | ✓ | ✓ |

181

Inverbeg Holiday Park, Inverbeg, by Luss, Dunbartonshire, G83 8PD
☎ *(Luss) 01436 860267*
15 acres, mixed, Mar-Oct, prior booking in peak periods, latest time of arrival 2300, overnight holding area. Extra charge for electricity, awnings.

50 tourers £6.50-7.50 or 50 motors £6.50-7.50 or 25 tents £6.50-7.50.
Total Touring Pitches 50.
12 Holiday Caravans to let, sleep 4-8 £70.00-350.00, total sleeping capacity 72, min. let 3 nights.

Leisure facilities:
Take M8 through Glasgow. Go over Erskine Bridge, take A82 for Crianlarich.
Park is 4 mls N of Luss on right hand side.

INVERGARRY, Inverness-shire, Map Ref. 3H11

30

Faichem Park, Ardgarry Farm, Faichem, Invergarry, Inverness-shire, PH35 4HG
☎ *(Invergarry) 01809 501226*
2 acres, mixed, Apr-Oct, prior booking in peak periods, latest time of arrival 2200.
Extra charge for showers.

15 tourers £5.50-6.00 or 15 motors £5.50-6.00 or 15 tents £5.50-6.00.
Total Touring Pitches 30.
Leisure facilities:
From A82 at Invergarry, take A87. Continue 1 ml, turn right at Faichem signpost, bear left up the hill and take first entrance on right.

INVERGLOY, by Spean Bridge, Inverness-shire, Map Ref. 3H11

INSPECTED

Booking Enquiries: Mrs M H Cairns, Invergloy House, Invergloy, by Spean Bridge, Inverness-shire, PH34 4DY
☎ *(Spean Bridge) 01397 712681*
2 Holiday Caravans to let, sleep 5 £170.00-225.00, total sleeping capacity 10, min.let 1/2 nights low season, Apr-Oct.

Leisure facilities:
5½ mls N of Spean Bridge on A82 to Inverness, enter at white fence on left, along 400 yds wooded drive.

Key to symbols
is on back flap

VAT is shown at 17.5%: changes in this rate may affect prices.

INVERMORISTON, Inverness-shire, Map Ref. 4A10

85

Loch Ness Caravan & Camping Park, Easter Port Clair, Invermoriston, Inverness-shire, IV3 6YE
☎ (Glenmoriston) 01320 351207
8 acres, grassy, stony, hard-standing, mid Mar-mid Oct, latest time of arrival 2130.
Extra charge for electricity, awnings.

50 tourers £6.00-9.00 or 50 motors £6.00-9.00 or 35 tents £5.50-8.50.
Total Touring Pitches 50.
5 Holiday Caravans to let, sleep 6 £120.00-200.00, total sleeping capacity 30, min. let 3 days.

Leisure facilities:
On A82 Inverness-Fort William ¾ ml from Invermoriston.

INVERNESS, Map Ref. 4B8

324

Bught Caravan & Camping Site, Inverness, IV3 5SR
☎ (Inverness) 01463 236920
1.8 acres, grassy, Apr-Oct, latest time of arrival 2200.
Extra charge for electricity, awnings.

90 tourers from £7.00 or 90 motors from £7.00 or 81 tents from £3.30.
Total Touring Pitches 171.
Site fully signposted from Inverness to Fort William road (A82).

50

Torvean Caravan Park, Glenurquhart Road, Inverness, IV3 6JL
☎ (Inverness) 01463 220582 Fax: 0186 282382
2 acres, grassy, level, sheltered, Easter-Oct, prior booking in peak periods, latest time of arrival 2000. Extra charge for electricity, awnings, showers.

50 tourers £7.50-8.00 or 50 motors £7.50-8.00. Total Touring Pitches 50. No tents.
10 Holiday Caravans to let, sleep 2-5 £215.00-295.00, total sleeping capacity 50, min. let 3 nights.

Leisure facilities:
From town centre take A82 signposted Fort William. Site is on outskirts of town, first right at canal bridge.

BY INVERNESS, Map Ref. 4B8

100

Bunchrew Caravan Park, Bunchrew, Inverness, IV3 6TD
☎ (Inverness) 01463 237802
20 acres, grassy, hard-standing, level, mid Mar-Dec, prior booking in peak periods, latest time of arrival 2200, overnight holding area. Extra charge for electricity, awnings.

100 tourers £7.00-7.50 or 100 motors £7.00-7.50 or 100 tents £7.00-7.50.
Total Touring Pitches 100.
9 Holiday Caravans to let, sleep 6 £135.00-215.00, total sleeping capacity 54, min. let 1 day.

Leisure facilities:
Take A862 (Beauly) road from Inverness for 3 mls. Park is on the shores of the Beauly Firth.

Important: Prices stated are estimates and may be subject to amendments

BY INVERNESS, Map Ref. 4B8

30

Scaniport Caravan & Camping Park, Scaniport, by Inverness, Inverness-shire, IV1 2DL
☎ *(Dores) 01463751 351*
2 acres, grassy, stony, Easter-Sep.

10 tourers £4.00-4.50 and 5 motors £4.00-4.50 and 15 tents £4.00-4.50.
Total Touring Pitches 30.
From Inverness take B862 SW towards Dores. Approx. 5 mls on.
Site is opposite telephone box at Scaniport.

INVERUGLAS, Dunbartonshire, Map Ref. 1G3

26

Loch Lomond Holiday Park, Inveruglas, Dunbartonshire, G83
☎ *(Inveruglas) 013014 224 Fax: 013014 224*
Booking Enquiries: Halley Caravans Ltd, Glasgow Road, Milngavie, Glasgow,
Dunbartonshire, G62 6JP
☎ *0141 956 1126 Fax: 0141 956 2361*
13 acres, hard-standing, level, Dec-Jan, Mar-Oct, prior booking in peak periods,
latest time of arrival 2200. Extra charge for electricity, awnings.

18 tourers £7.00-10.00 or 18 motors £7.00-10.00. Total Touring Pitches 18. No tents.
13 Holiday Caravans to let, sleep 6 £130.00-285.00, total sleeping capacity 78,
min. let 3 days.

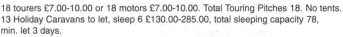

Leisure facilities: ⚓ 🎾 🎣
From Dumbarton take A82 N following W side of Loch Lomond. Take right fork at
Tarbet Hotel, park is on Lochside, 3½ mls N of Tarbet.

JEDBURGH Roxburghshire, Map Ref. 2E7

65

Jedwater Caravan Park, Jedburgh, Roxburghshire, TD8 6QS
☎ *(Camptown) 01835 840219 Fax: 01835 840219*
10 acres, grassy, level, sheltered, mixed, Apr-Oct, prior booking in peak periods,
latest time of arrival 2300, overnight holding area. Extra charge for electricity, awnings.

65 tourers £8.00-9.00 or 65 motors £8.00-9.00 or 65 tents £7.00-8.00.
Total Touring Pitches 65.
5 Holiday Caravans to let, sleep 2-8 £130.00-280.00, total sleeping capacity 34,
min. let 2 nights.

Leisure facilities: 🏓 ⚓ 🎾 ⛳ 🎣 🎿
From Jedburgh take A68 S for 3 mls. Turn left at sign, 6 mls N of Carter Bar.

130

Lilliardsedge Park, Jedburgh, Roxburghshire, TD8 6TZ
☎ *(Ancrum) 01835 830271*
25 acres, grassy, stony, Easter-Sep, prior booking in peak periods, latest time of arrival 22.30.
Extra charge for electricity, awnings, showers.

25 tourers £7.50-8.00 and 5 motors £7.50-8.00 and 10 tents £7.50-8.00.
Total Touring Pitches 40.
2 Holiday Caravans to let, sleep 4 £140.00-190.00, total sleeping capacity 8,
min. let weekend.

On A68, 5 mls N of Jedburgh.

Key to symbols
is on back flap

JOHN O'GROATS, Caithness, Map Ref. 4E2

John o' Groats, John O'Groats, Caithness, KW1 4YR
☎ *(John O'Groats) 0195581 329*
3 acres, mixed, Apr-Oct. Extra charge for electricity, awnings, showers.

🛉 🕯 ☉ 📷 ✦ 🗮 ⌨ wc 🅿 🐕 ☂ ✕ 🏇 🛆 🍴 🎯 🅳

45 tourers £5.50-6.50 or 45 motors £5.50-6.50 or 45 tents £5.50-6.50.
Total Touring Pitches 45.
Leisure facilities: 🥾 🦆 ∪
Site is at end of A9 on seafront, beside the Last House in Scotland.

JOHNSHAVEN, Kincardineshire, Map Ref. 4G12

Wairds Park Caravan Site, Beach Road, Johnshaven, Kincardineshire, DD10 0HD
☎ *(Inverbervie) 01561 362280/362395*
Booking Enquiries: Mrs E Adam, 2 Herd Crescent, Johnshaven,
Kincardineshire, DD10 0EZ
☎ *(Inverbervie) 01561 362616*
6 acres, grassy, sandy, sheltered, Apr-mid Oct, prior booking in peak periods,
latest time of arrival 2000, overnight holding area. Extra charge for awnings.

🛉 🕯 ☉ 📷 ✦ 🍴 ⌨ 🅿 🐕 ☂ ✕ 🏇 🛖 🛆 🍴 🅳

20 tourers £6.00-7.00 or 20 motors £6.00-7.00 or 20 tents £5.00-6.00.
Total Touring Pitches 20.
Leisure facilities: 🏐 ⚲
From Montrose take A92 for 9 mls, turn right at Johnshaven road end.
From Stonehaven take A92 for 15 mls. Turn left at Johnshaven road end.

Important: Prices stated are estimates and may be subject to amendments

KENMORE, Perthshire, Map Ref. 2A1

Kenmore Caravan and Camping Park

By Aberfeldy PH15 2HN
Tel: (01887) 830226 Fax: (01887) 830211

Pleasant site by the River Tay. Many beautiful forest or mountain walks. Ideal touring centre. Abundant wildlife. Jeep safaris. An excellent golf course adjacent to park (par 70, 6500 yards) with discount green fees to residents; others nearby. Fishing on the river or Loch Tay. Most other water activities. A recreational field, two children's play areas and a dog activity area. Pony trekking and leisure complex with pool in Aberfeldy. Electric points, bar food in our own Byre Bistro and a variety of places to eat well at locally. The site is quiet at night and owner-supervised.

D. Menzies and Partners.

220

Kenmore Caravan & Camping Park, Kenmore, Aberfeldy, Perthshire, PH15 2HN
☎ *(Kenmore) 01887 830226 Fax: 01887 830211*
14 acres, grassy, level, sloping, Mar-Oct, prior booking in peak periods, latest time of arrival 2230, overnight holding area. Extra charge for electricity, awnings.

60 tourers £7.00-8.00 and 10 motors £7.00-8.00 and 90 tents £6.00-7.00.
Total Touring Pitches 160.
Holiday Caravan to let, sleeps 6 £100.00-275.00.

Leisure facilities:
From Ballinluig on A827 W to Loch Tay. From Killin on A827 E to Kenmore.
From Crieff on A822 N to Aberfeldy.

KILBARCHAN, Renfrewshire, Map Ref. 1H5

15

Barnbrock Camping Site, Barnbrock Farm, Kilbarchan, Renfrewshire, PA10 2PZ
☎ *(Bridge of Weir) 01505 614791*
Booking Enquiries: Clyde Muirshiel Regional Park, Barnbrock Farm, Kilbarchan, Renfrewshire, PA10 2PZ
☎ *(Bridge of Weir) 01505 614791*
5 acres, grassy, Apr-Nov, latest time of arrival 2100.

30 tents £2.00-4.00. Total Touring Pitches 30. No tourers, motorvans.
Leisure facilities:
Take B786, Kilmacolm road, from Lochwinnoch, for 4 mls.
Turn right onto unclassified road. Site 100 yds on right.

Key to symbols
is on back flap

KILBERRY, by Tarbert, Argyll, Map Ref. 1D5

Port Ban Caravan Park, Kilberry, Tarbert, Argyll, PA29 6YD
☎ *(Ormsary) 018803 224*
12 acres, mixed, Apr-Oct, prior booking in peak periods, latest time of arrival 2300.
Extra charge for electricity, awnings, showers.

🛆 🏳 ☉ 🗔 ✄ 🕮 E 🅦 🄿 🖰 ✕ 🐎 🎠 ⚠ 🆁 🛋 ♨ 🛆 🔌 🍴 ✗

30 tourers £5.30-8.80 or 30 motors £5.30-8.80 or 30 tents £5.30-8.80.
Total Touring Pitches 30.
12 Holiday Caravans to let, sleep 6-8 from £85.00, total sleeping capacity 96,
min. let 1 night.

🛆 🏳 ☉ E 🅦 🄿 🖰 ✕ 🐎 🎠 ⚠ 🔌 🍴 🛆 ✗

Leisure facilities: 🎣 🌐 ⚲ 🚣 △ ⚓

From Glasgow follow signs for Lochgilphead on A82/A83 road. 4 mls beyond
Lochgilphead turn right on to B8024. Carry on for 14 mls. Site 1 ml before Kilberry.

KILCHOAN, by Ardnamurchan, Argyll, Map Ref. 1C1

Booking Enquiries: Mrs C G Cameron, Mo Dhachaidh, Portuairk,
Kilchoan, by Ardnamurchan, Argyll, PH36 4LN
☎ *(Kilchoan) 01972 510285*
Holiday Caravan to let, sleeps 6 £100.00-160.00, min.let weekend, Apr-Oct.

🛆 🏳 ☉ E 🅦 🄿 🖰 ✕ 🐎 🎠 🍴 🔌 🍴 🛆 🚜

KINTORE, Aberdeenshire, Map Ref. 4G10

Hillhead Caravan Park, Kintore, Aberdeenshire, AB51 0YX
☎ *(Kintore) 01467 632809 Fax: 01467 633173*
Booking Enquiries: Mr L Gray
11/2 acres, grassy, level, Apr-Oct, prior booking in peak periods, latest time of arrival 2200.
Extra charge for electricity.

🛆 🏳 ☉ 🗔 ✄ 🍴 🕮 🅦 🄿 🛒 🖰 ✕ 🐎 ⚠ 🛋 🛆 🔌 🍴 🎫

24 tourers £5.30-6.75 or 24 motors £5.30-6.75 or 24 tents £5.30-6.75.
Total Touring Pitches 24.
5 Holiday Caravans to let, sleep 6 £95.00-235.00, total sleeping capacity 30,
min. let 1 night.

🛆 🏳 ☉ 🍴 🖵 E 🅦 🄿 🛒 🖰 ✕ 🐎 ⚠ 🍴 🔌 🍴 🛆 🎫 🄳

Leisure facilities: 🌐 ▶ 🎣

A96 Aberdeen-Kintore, left via Ratch Hill. In 1/2 ml left via Blairs. Park on left.
Or follow signs from A96-B994 for 2 mls. Right via Kintore. Park is 1 ml on right.

GRADING
YOUR GUARANTEE
OF QUALITY

KIPPFORD, Kirkcudbrightshire, Map Ref. 2B10

KIPPFORD CARAVAN PARK
Kippford, by Dalbeattie
Kirkcudbrightshire DG5 4LF
Tel: (01556) 620636

THISTLE AWARD family owned holiday park, in undulating part-wooded setting, landscaped with specimen trees and shrubs. Top quality caravans and bungalows for sale or hire, fully serviced with colour TV and fridge. Launderette. Tents and tourers. Electric hook up available. Adventure playground and junior play area. Shop and phone 20 yards. Pony trekking, golf, fishing, sailing, cycling and seaside all within 2 miles.

★ *Brochure by return.* ✓ ✓ ✓ ✓ ✓

Kippford Caravan Park, Kippford, Kirkcudbrightshire, DG5 4LF
☎ *(Kippford) 01556 620636*
18 acres, mixed, Mar-Oct, prior booking in peak periods, latest time of arrival 2400, overnight holding area. Extra charge for electricity, awnings.

45 tourers £7.00-9.00 or 45 motors £7.00-9.00 or 45 tents £4.00-9.00. Total Touring Pitches 45.
16 Holiday Caravans to let, sleep 4-8 £65.00-300.00, total sleeping capacity 96, min. let weekend.

Leisure facilities: ☉ ⵀ ♪ ⚲ ∪ ⬦
From Dalbeattie take A710 S for 4 mls. Site on right just past turning to Kippford.

KIRKCALDY, Fife, Map Ref. 2D4

Dunnikier Caravan Park, Dunnikier Way, Kirkcaldy, Fife, KY1 3ND
☎ *(Kirkcaldy) 01592 267563*
7 acres, grassy, hard-standing, level, Mar-Jan, latest time of arrival 1800.

60 tourers £6.00-8.00 or 60 motors £6.00-8.00 or 20 tents £4.00-6.00. Total Touring Pitches 60.
Exit M90 at Jnc 3 and take A92 to Kirkcaldy West.

QUALITY
AT ITS BEST.
THISTLE AWARD

Key to symbols is on back flap

VAT is shown at 17.5%: changes in this rate may affect prices.

KIRKCUDBRIGHT , Map Ref. 2A11

BRIGHOUSE BAY HOLIDAY PARK
3 Borgue Road, Kirkcudbright DG6 4TS
Telephone: (01557) 7267   Fax: (01557) 7319

Scottish AA 'Campsight of Year'. Premier park hidden away within 700 coastal acres. Exceptional leisure facilities. Indoor pool, jacuzzi, sunbed, Turkish room, toddlers corner, fitness suite, lounge, bistro, games room, 9-hole golf course, watersports, slipway, beach, open farm, pony trekking. Lodges/luxury caravans sale and rent. Family camping. *OPEN ALL YEAR.*

240

Brighouse Bay Holiday Park, Borgue Road, Kirkcudbright, DG6 4TS
☎ *(Borgue)* 015577 267
25 acres, mixed, Jan-Dec, prior booking in peak periods, latest time of arrival 2130, overnight holding area. Extra charge for electricity, awnings.

120 tourers £8.50-10.50 or 120 motors £8.50-10.50 or 120 tents £8.50-10.50.
Total Touring Pitches 120.
25 Holiday Caravans to let, sleep 4-8 £120.00-325.00, total sleeping capacity 160, min. let 2 nights.

Leisure facilities:
From Kirkcudbright take A755 W for ¹/₂ ml, turn left on to B727 signposted Borgue. After 4 mls turn left signposted Brighouse Bay. Park on right of bay behind wood in 2 mls.

50

Seaward Caravan Park, Dhoon Bay, Kirkcudbright, DG6 4TJ
☎ *(Kirkcudbright)* 01557 331079
Booking Enquiries: Seaward Caravan Park, c/o Booking Office, Brighouse Bay, Kirkcudbright, DG6 4TS
☎ *(Borgue)* 015577 267
6¹/₂ acres, mixed, Mar-Oct, prior booking in peak periods, latest time of arrival 2130, overnight holding area. Extra charge for electricity, awnings.

20 tourers £7.00-9.50 or 20 motors £7.00-9.50 or 20 tents £7.00-9.50.
Total Touring Pitches 20.
11 Holiday Caravans to let, sleep 4-8 £140.00-300.00, total sleeping capacity 77, min. let 2 nights.

Leisure facilities:
From Kirkcudbright take A755 W for ¹/₂ ml. turn left onto B727, signposted Borgue. Park is on right in 2 mls.

KIRKWALL, Orkney, Map Ref. 5B11

30

Pickaquoy Caravan & Camping Site, Pickaquoy Road, Kirkwall, Orkney, KW15 1RR
Booking Enquiries: Education Department, County Offices, School Place, Kirkwall, Orkney, KW15 1JG
☎ *(Kirkwall)* 01856 873535
2 acres, grassy, sandy, May-Sep. Extra charge for electricity, awnings, showers.

30 tourers to £4.50 or 30 motors to £4.50 or 30 tents £2.10-3.90.
Total Touring Pitches 30.

Leisure facilities: ✦
Turn right on leaving ferry, follow A965 to Kirkwall, turn off right before entering town (signposted).

LAIRG, Sutherland, Map Ref. 4A6

60

Dunroamin Caravan Park, Main Street, Lairg, Sutherland, IV27 4AR
☎ *(Lairg) 01549 402447*
2¹/₂ acres, grassy, hard-standing, level, Apr-Oct, latest time of arrival 2300, overnight holding area. Extra charge for electricity, awnings, showers.

20 tourers £4.50-6.00 and 20 motors £4.50-6.00 and 20 tents £4.50-5.50.
Total Touring Pitches 60.
9 Holiday Caravans to let, sleep 6 £75.00-245.00, total sleeping capacity 54, min. let 1 night.

Leisure facilities:
On A839, Main Street, Lairg, behind Crofters Restaurant.

60

Woodend Caravan & Camping Site, Achnairn, Lairg, Sutherland, IV27 4DN
☎ *(Lairg) 01549 402248*
4 acres, mixed, Apr-Sep, latest time of arrival 2300.
Extra charge for electricity, showers.

53 tourers £5.00-5.50 or 53 motors £5.00-5.50 or 53 tents £5.00-5.50.
Total Touring Pitches 53.
5 Holiday Caravans to let, sleep 6 £120.00-130.00, total sleeping capacity 30, min. let weekend (2 nights).

From Lairg take A836 N 3 mls to AA kiosk, turn left onto A838 then first right. Site signs at AA kiosk.

LANARK, Map Ref. 2B6

45

Newhouse Caravan & Camping Park, Ravenstruther, Lanark, ML11 8NP
☎ *(Carstairs) 01555 870228*
4 acres, mixed, Mar-Oct, latest time of arrival 2200, overnight holding area.
Extra charge for electricity, awnings, showers.

25 tourers £6.00-7.00 or 25 motors £6.00-7.00 or 25 tents £5.00-7.00.
Total Touring Pitches 45.
4 Holiday Caravans to let, sleep 2-6 £130.00-200.00, total sleeping capacity 20, min. let 3 days.

Leisure facilities:
Site on A70, ¹/₂ ml W of Carstairs village, 3 mls E of Lanark.

LANGHOLM, Dumfriesshire, Map Ref. 2D9

12

Whiteshiels Caravan Park, Langholm, Dumfriesshire, DG13
☎ *(Langholm) 013873 80494*
2/3 acres, mixed, Jan-Dec, latest time of arrival 2200, overnight holding area.
Extra charge for electricity, awnings.

12 tourers £6.00-6.50 or 12 motors £5.00-5.50 or 12 tents £5.00-5.50.
Total Touring Pitches 12.
Leisure facilities:
A7 road ¹/₂ ml N of Langholm turn in at cafe on left. Entrance at back of cafe.

Key to symbols is on back flap

LAURENCEKIRK, Kincardineshire, Map Ref. 4G12

Dovecot Caravan Park, North Water Bridge, Laurencekirk, Kincardineshire, AB30 1QL
☎ *(Northwaterbridge) 01674 840630*
Booking Enquiries: Mrs A Mowatt
6 acres, grassy, sheltered, Apr-Oct, latest time of arrival 2000, overnight holding area. Extra charge for electricity, awnings.

🛠 🐾 ☉ 🗗 ⚡ 🛆 🕼 ☐ 🆆🅲 🅿 ⟳ ✕ 🐕 ⚠ 🎣 ☖ 🚗 🚻

25 tourers £6.00-7.00 or 25 motors £6.00-7.00 or 25 tents £6.00-7.00.
Total Touring Pitches 25.
2 Holiday Caravans to let, sleep 6-8 £120.00-140.00, total sleeping capacity 14.

🛠 🐾 ☐ 🆆🅲 🅿 ⟳ ✕ 🐕 ⚠ ⊘ ☖ 🔥 🅳

Leisure facilities: 🎱 🏌
From Laurencekirk (A90) 5 mls S at Northwater Bridge, turn right to Edzell.
Site is 300 mtrs on left.

LAXDALE, Lewis, Western Isles, Map Ref. 3D4

Laxdale Holiday Park, 6 Laxdale Lane, Laxdale, Lewis, Western Isles, PA86
☎ *(Stornoway) 01851 703234*
Booking Enquiries: Mr D Macleod, 4 Laxdale Lane, Laxdale, Lewis, Western Isles, PA86 0DR
☎ *(Stornoway) 01851 703234*
2½ acres, grassy, sloping, sheltered, Apr-Oct, latest time of arrival 2400.
Extra charge for electricity, awnings, showers.

🛠 🐾 🕼 E 🆆🅲 🅿 🛒 ✕ 🐕 ☖ 🚗 🚻

6 tourers to £7.00 and 6 motors to £7.00 and 37 tents to £6.00. Total Touring Pitches 49.
3 Holiday Caravans to let, sleep 4-6 £100.00-180.00, total sleeping capacity 18, min. let weekend.

🅼 🛠 🐾 ☉ 🛆 ☐ E 🆆🅲 🅿 🛒 ✕ 🐕 🚗 ⊘ ☖ 🔥 🅳

From Stornoway (ferry terminal) take the A857 for 2 mls to Laxdale.

TELEPHONE DIALLING CODES

On 16 April 1995 all UK area codes starting **0** will start **01**.

From August 1994 until 16 April 1995, the new codes will be run in parallel with the old ones.
If you experience difficulty in connecting a call, please call Directory Enquiries – **192** – for advice. Please note: A charge will be made for this service when using a private phone.

LINLITHGOW, West Lothian, Map Ref. 2B5

Beecraigs Caravan Park
Beecraigs Country Park, near Linlithgow
Telephone: (01506) 844516

Situated two miles south of Linlithgow within the award winning Beecraigs Country Park, this site offers attractive, secluded, fully serviced landscaped bays with modern toilet and shower blocks, all suitable for the disabled. Leisure facilities within the park include a restaurant, childrens play areas, barbecue sites, country walks, outdoor activities (bookable in advance) and angling by permit. There are also trout and deer farms to visit. The nearby town of Linlithgow, birthplace of Mary Queen of Scots, offers a unique combination of historical attractions and a variety of shopping, all within easy reach of Beecraigs. *Contact: P. Sutherland.*

★ **TENTS £5.50-£7.50 per night.**
★ **TOURERS from £7-£8 per night.**

★ 1994 prices ★

Beecraigs Caravan Park, Linlithgow, West Lothian, EH49 6PL
☎ *(Linlithgow)* 01506 844516 Fax: 01506 847824
Booking Enquiries: Park Centre, Beecraigs Caravan Park, Linlithgow, West Lothian, EH49 6PL

56

1000 acres, grassy, hard-standing, sheltered, Jan-Dec, prior booking in peak periods, latest time of arrival 2100, overnight holding area. Extra charge for electricity, awnings.

39 tourers £7.00-8.00 or 39 motors £7.00-8.00 or 35 tents £5.50-7.50.
Total Touring Pitches 39.
Leisure facilities:
From M9 leave motorway for Linlithgow. Follow signs Beecraigs Country Park.
From M8 leave motorway for Bathgate. Follow B792 until signs for Beecraigs.

Key to symbols is on back flap

VAT is shown at 17.5%: changes in this rate may affect prices.

LOCHGILPHEAD, Argyll, Map Ref. 1E4

Castle Sween Bay Holidays

Ellary, Lochgilphead, Argyll PA31 8PA
Telephone: (01880) 770209/770232
Fax: (018803) 386
What do you look for in a Caravan Park?
* Attractive rural setting?
* Easy relaxed atmosphere?
* Friendly and efficient staff?
* First-class amenities?
    (Bar, shop, restaurant etc.)
* Grounds kept up to a high standard?
Castle Sween comes out top in every respect.
Enquiries to Castle Sween Bay (Holidays),
Ellary, Lochgilphead, Argyll.
Tel. (01880) 770209/770232
or (0154685) 223.

200

Castle Sween Bay Holidays Ltd, Ellary, Lochgilphead, Argyll, PA31 8BP
☎ *(Achnamara)* 0154685 223
Booking Enquries: Tel: 01880 770209/770232.
120 acres, grassy, level, sheltered, Mar-Oct, prior booking in peak periods.

20 Holiday Caravans to let, sleep 4-6 £155.00-310.00, total sleeping capacity 120,
min. let 2 nights, Mar-Oct.

Leisure facilities:
Leave Lochgilphead on the A816 (Oban), turn left at Cairnbaan onto the B814
(Crinan) and left again at Bellanoch. Follow signs.

70

Lochgilphead Caravan Site, Lochgilphead, Argyll, PA31
☎ *(Lochgilphead)* 01546 602003 Fax: 01546 603699
6³/₄ acres, grassy, hard-standing, level, sheltered, Apr-Oct, overnight holding area.
Extra charge for electricity, awnings.

30 tourers from £6.50 or 30 motors from £6.50 or 10 tents from £6.50.
Total Touring Pitches 40.
15 Holiday Caravans to let, sleep 4-6 from £100.00, total sleeping capacity 80,
min. let 2 nights.

Leisure facilities:
Within town of Lochgilphead. Close to junction of A83 and A816.

LOCKERBIE, Dumfriesshire, Map Ref. 2C9

70

Halleaths Caravan Park, Lockerbie, Dumfriesshire, DG11 1LS
☎ *(Dumfries)* 01387 810630
8 acres, mixed, Mar-Nov, prior booking in peak periods, latest time of arrival 2200,
overnight holding area. Extra charge for electricity, awnings, showers.

50 tourers £6.00 or 20 motors £6.00 or 20 tents £5.00. Total Touring Pitches 70.
From Lockerbie on A74 take A709 to Lochmaben, Park is ¹/₂ ml on right after
crossing River Annan.

LONGNIDDRY, East Lothian, Map Ref. 2D5

628

Seton Sands Holiday Village, Longniddry, East Lothian, EH32 0QF
☎ *(Port Seton) 01875 813333*
Booking Enquiries: Bourne Leisure Group Ltd, Seton Sands Holiday Village,
Longniddry, East Lothian, EH32 0QF
☎ *(Port Seton) 01875 813333/(0442)48661*
52 acres, grassy, sandy, level, Mar-Oct, prior booking in peak periods,
latest time of arrival 2200, overnight holding area. Extra charge for electricity.

60 tourers £8.75-10.75 or 60 motors £8.75-10.75. Total Touring Pitches 60.
No tents.
150 Holiday Caravans to let, sleep 6-8 £48.00-399.00, total sleeping capacity 942,
min. let 1 night.

Leisure facilities:
From the Tranent r/about, turn on to the B6731 for Cockenzie, then right on the
B1348. The park is 1 ml along on the right.

Seton Sands Holiday Centre
Booking Enquiries: Mrs N Butler, 35 High Street, Markinch, Fife, KY7 6DQ
☎ *(Glenrothes) 01592 757428*
Holiday Caravan to let, sleeps 6 £90.00-260.00, min.let 2 days, mid Mar-Oct.

Leisure facilities:
From the A1, at Tranent roundabout, turn onto B6371 for Cockenzie,
then right onto B1348. Park is 1 ml on right.

LOSSIEMOUTH, Moray, Map Ref. 4D7

505

**Silver Sands Leisure Park, Covesea, West Beach, Lossiemouth,
Moray, IV31 6SP**
☎ *(Lossiemouth) 01343 813262 Fax: 01343 815205*
55 acres, grassy, sandy, level, Apr-Oct, prior booking in peak periods, latest time of
arrival 2300, overnight holding area. Extra charge for electricity, awnings.

140 tourers £7.50-9.50 or 140 motors £7.50-9.50 or 140 tents £7.50-9.50.
Total Touring Pitches 140.
55 Holiday Caravans to let, sleep 4-8 £130.00-420.00, total sleeping capacity 350,
min. let 2 nights.

Leisure facilities:
A941 Elgin, towards Lossiemouth first left for RAF camp, past camp to T-junction.
Left for Covesea lighthouse (1 ml). Park on right by lighthouse.

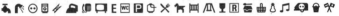

Key to symbols
is on back flap

LUNDIN LINKS, Fife, Map Ref. 2D3

25

Woodland Gardens Caravan & Camping Site, Blindwell Road, Lundin Links, Fife, KY8 5QG
☎ *(Upper Largo) 01333 360319*
1 acre, mixed, Mar-Oct, prior booking in peak periods, latest time of arrival 2200, overnight holding area. Extra charge for electricity, awnings.

🔪 🐾 ☉ 🖩 ✄ 🛢 🐷 🖵 E 🆆 P 💺 ♻ ✕ 🐎 🏛 🏔 🏚 🛇 🍴 ♿

20 tourers £5.40 or 20 motors £5.40 or 20 tents £5.40. Total Touring Pitches 20.
4 Holiday Caravans to let, sleep 6-9 £95.00-250.00, total sleeping capacity 27, min. let 2 nights.

🔪 🐾 ☉ 🛢 🖵 E 🆆 P 💺 ♻ ✕ 🐎 🏛 🏔 🛖 🛇 🍴 ♿

Leisure facilities: 🎣
At E end of Lundin Links, turn N off A915 for ½ ml. Site signposted.

LUSS, Dunbartonshire, Map Ref. 1G4

90

Camping & Caravanning Club Site, Luss Camping Ground, Luss, Dunbartonshire, G83 8NT
☎ *(Luss) 0143686 658*
Booking Enquiries: The Camping & Caravanning Club, Greenfields House, Westwood Way, Coventry, CV4 8JH
☎ *(Coventry) 01203 694995 (out of season)* Fax: 01203 694886 (out of season)
12 acres, grassy, level, Mar-Oct, prior booking in peak periods, latest time of arrival 2100, overnight holding area. Extra charge for electricity.

🔪 🐾 🖩 🆆 P ♻ ✕ 🐎 🏔 🛇 🍴 £

90 motors £6.62-7.41 or 90 tents £6.62-7.41. Total Touring Pitches 90. No tourers.
Leisure facilities: ☯
The site is on the lochside ¼ ml N of village of Luss on A82 Glasgow-Fort William road. It lies between the road and Loch Lomond.

MACHRIHANISH, by Campbeltown, Argyll, Map Ref. 1D8

100

Camping & Caravanning Club Site, East Trodigal, Machrihanish, Campbeltown, Argyll, PA28 6PT
☎ *(Machrihanish) 0158681 366*
Booking Enquiries: The Camping & Caravanning Club, Greenfields House, Westwood Way, Coventry, CV4 8JH
☎ *(Coventry) 01203 694995 (out of season)* Fax: 01203 694886 (out of season)
10 acres, mixed, Mar-Sep, prior booking in peak periods, latest time of arrival 2100, overnight holding area. Extra charge for electricity.

🔪 🐾 ☉ 🖩 ✄ 🛢 🖩 P 💺 ♻ ✕ 🐎 🏔 🍽 🍲 🛖 🛇 🍴 ♿ 🦯 £ D

90 tourers £5.50-6.18 or 90 motors £5.50-6.18 or 90 tents £5.50-6.18.
Total Touring Pitches 90.
A82 from Glasgow to Tarbet. Then A83 to Campbeltown. From town take B843 (to Machrihanish). Site is on N side of road ½ ml before Machrihanish.

MANISH, Harris, Western Isles, Map Ref. 3B7

INSPECTED

Booking Enquiries: Mrs Sheila MacLeod, 8 Lower Manish, Manish, Harris, Western Isles, PA85 3EZ
☎ *(Manish) 01859 530305*
Holiday Caravan to let, sleeps 4 to £75.00, min. let weekend, Jan-Dec.

Ⓜ 🔪 🐾 ☉ 🛢 E 🆆 P 💺 ♻ ✕ 🐎 🏔 🛖 ◎ 🛇 🛏 Ⓣ 🦽

Leisure facilities: 🎿 🦆 ⛵

MAYBOLE, Ayrshire, Map Ref. 1G8

75

Camping & Caravanning Club Site, Culzean Castle, Glenside, by Maybole, Ayrshire, KA19 8JL
☎ *(Kirkoswald) 016556 627*
Booking Enquiries: The Camping & Caravanning Club, Greenfields House, Westwood Way, Coventry, CV4 8JH
☎ *(Coventry) 01203 694995 (out of season) Fax: 01203 694886 (out of season)*
6 acres, grassy, hard-standing, Mar-Oct, prior booking in peak periods, latest time of arrival 2100, overnight holding area. Extra charge for electricity.

🏕 ♟ ☉ ⬛ 🛁 🛒 🏢 E ᵂᶜ 🅿 🅖 ✕ 🐕 Ⓜ ♨ ⍦ 🎙 🍴 🔁 Ⓓ

90 tourers £6.62-7.41 or 90 motors £6.62-7.41 or 90 tents £6.62-7.41.
Total Touring Pitches 90.
Entrance to site as for entrance to Culzean Castle, off A719.
Regular bus service from Ayr passes the entrance.

MELVICH, Sutherland, Map Ref. 4B3

14

Croft Inn Caravan Park, Melvich, by Thurso
☎ *(Melvich) 016413 262/01641 531262*
Booking Enquiries: Mrs J Ritchie, 81 Melvich, by Thurso
☎ *(Melvich) 016413 262/01461 531262*
1/3 acres, grassy, hard-standing, Apr-Sep, prior booking in peak periods, latest time of arrival 1800. Extra charge for awnings, showers.

🏕 ♟ ☉ ⬛ ⚡ 🛒 🏢 E ᵂᶜ 🅿 🛒 🅖 ✕ 🍴 Ⓡ ☕ ♨ ♪ ⍦ 🍴 🔁 Ⓓ

4 tourers £6.00-10.00 and 4 motors £6.00-10.00 and 6 tents £5.00-8.00.
Total Touring Pitches 14.
Leisure facilities: ♦ ► ✈ ✦ ∪ ✓
On main A836 Thurso/Tongue road beside Croft Inn.

MOFFAT, Dumfriesshire, Map Ref. 2C8

200

Camping & Caravanning Club Site, Hammerland's Farm, Moffat, Dumfriesshire, DG10 9QL
☎ *(Moffat) 01683 20436*
Booking Enquiries: The Camping & Caravanning Club, Greenfields House, Westwood Way, Coventry, CV4 8JH
☎ *(Coventry) 01203 694995 (out of season) Fax: 01203 694886 (out of season)*
12 acres, grassy, level, sheltered, Mar-Oct, prior booking in peak periods, latest time of arrival 2100, overnight holding area. Extra charge for electricity.

🏕 ♟ ☉ ⬛ ⚡ 🛒 🏢 E ᵂᶜ 🅿 🛒 🅖 ✕ 🐕 Ⓜ ♨ ⍦ 🍴 🔁 Ⓓ

200 tourers £6.62-7.41 or 200 motors £6.62-7.41 or 200 tents £6.62-7.41.
Total Touring Pitches 200.
Take A708 NE from Moffat. Site approach is on right, before Caspers Inn.
Turn left at Cadet Hut, then left over bridge. Follow the signs.

Key to symbols is on back flap

VAT is shown at 17.5%: changes in this rate may affect prices.

MONTROSE, Angus, Map Ref. 2E1

Littlewood Holiday Park, Brechin Road, Montrose, Angus, DD10 9LE
☎ *(Montrose) 01674 672973*
3¹/₂ acres, grassy, level, Jan-Dec (Vans), Apr-Oct (Tour), prior booking in peak periods, periods, latest time of arrival 2300. Extra charge for electricity.

10 tourers £7.00-8.00 or 10 motors £7.00-8.00. Total Touring Pitches 10. No tents.
5 Holiday Caravans to let, sleep 6 £130.00-235.00, total sleeping capacity 30, min. let 2 nights.

Leisure facilities: ✪ ► ✔ ✔ U ✓
Through Montrose towards Aberdeen, turn left along A935 at last set of traffic lights. Park is 1 ml on left.

South Links Caravan Park, Traill Drive, Montrose, Angus, DD10
☎ *(Montrose) 01674 672026 (office hours)*
Booking Enquiries: Montrose Swimming Pool, The Mall, Montrose, Angus, DD10 8NN
☎ *(Montrose) 01674 672026*
10³/₄ acres, grassy, sloping, Apr-early Oct, prior booking in peak periods, latest time of arrival 2100. Extra charge for electricity.

172 tourers £7.70-8.85 or 172 motors £7.70-8.85 or 172 tents £3.45-4.60.
Total Touring Pitches 172.
E of A92, follow signs to beach – Traill Drive.

Tayock Caravan Park, Brechin Road, Montrose, Angus, DD10 9LE
☎ *(Montrose) 0674 673253*
41/2 acres, Apr-Oct, prior booking in peak periods, latest time of arrival 2200.

4 Holiday Caravans to let, sleep 6 £120.00-240.00, total sleeping capacity 24, min. let weekend, Apr-Oct.

1 ml W of Montrose on A935.

MUASDALE, by Tarbert, Argyll, Map Ref. 1D6

Muasdale Holiday Park, Muasdale, by Tarbert, Argyll, PA29 6XD
☎ *(Glenbarr) 015832 207/01546 602003 Fax: 01546 603699*
3/4 acre, grassy, Apr-Oct, latest time of arrival 2300, overnight holding area. Extra charge for electricity, awnings.

20 tourers from £5.00 or 20 motors from £5.00 or 20 tents from £5.00.
Total Touring Pitches 20.
8 Holiday Caravans to let, sleep 6 from £100.00, total sleeping capacity 48, min. let weekend.

Leisure facilities: ✦ ►
From Tarbert (Loch Fyne) take A83 towards Campbeltown.
Site at village of Muasdale (23 mls).

MUNLOCHY, Ross-shire, Map Ref. 4A8

INSPECTED

Booking Enquiries: Mrs J MacLeod, Knockbain Mains, Munlochy, Ross-shire, IV8 8PG
☎ *(Munlochy) 01463 811292*
Holiday Caravan to let, sleeps 6 £85.00-120.00, min. let 1 night, Apr-Oct.

🔥 ⁂ ⌂ ⌷ E ⧫ 🄿 ↻ ⛺ 🏭 ⚠ 🚩 ⬚ ⬚ ⬚ ⬚

Follow A9 to Tore r/bout, take A9 to Wick 400 metres turn right, signposted Killen.
2 mls to X roads, turn left. 1 ml on left to Knockbain Mains, sign to farmhouse.

MUSSELBURGH, East Lothian, Map Ref. 2D5

120

Drummohr Caravan Park, Levenhall, Musselburgh, East Lothian, EH21 8JS
☎ *0131 665 6867 Fax: 0131 653 6859*
10 acres, mixed, prior booking in peak periods, latest time of arrival 2200,
overnight holding area. Extra charge for electricity, awnings, showers.

🔥 ⁂ ⊙ ⬚ ⚡ ⌂ ⬚ E ⧫ 🄿 ↻ ✕ ⛺ ⚠ ⬚ ⬚ ⬚ ⬚

90 tourers £7.50-8.50 or 90 motors £7.50-8.50 or 30 tents £7.50-8.50.
Total Touring Pitches 120.

Leisure facilities: ⊕

1½ mls E of Musselburgh between B1348 Prestonpans and B1361 North Berwick road.

NAIRN, Map Ref. 4C8

DELNIES WOODS CARAVAN PARK
Delnies Woods, Nairn IV1 5NT
Telephone: 01667 455281   **Fax: 01667 455437**

Family run, highly acclaimed park, set in a conifer wood right in
the heart of the Highlands. Secluded pitches for tourers, tents,
motorhomes. Luxury holiday caravans for hire. Ideal centre for
touring the Highlands. Located between Loch Ness and the
Whisky Trail.   *2 miles west of Nairn on A96*

78

Delnies Woods Caravan Park, Delnies Woods, Nairn, IV12 5NT
☎ *(Nairn) 01667 455281 Fax: 01667 455437*
10 acres, mixed, Easter-Oct, prior booking in peak periods, overnight holding area.
Extra charge for electricity.

🔥 ⁂ ⊙ ⬚ ⌂ ⬚ ⌷ E ⧫ 🄿 ⚡ ↻ ✕ ⛺ ⚠ ⬚ ⬚ ⬚ ⬚ ⬚ ⬚

50 tourers £6.00-8.00 or 50 motors £6.00-8.00 or 20 tents £6.00.
Total Touring Pitches 70.
6 Holiday Caravans to let, sleep 6-8 £100.00-275.00, total sleeping capacity 38,
min. let weekend.

⚠ ⬚ ⬚ ⬚ ⬚ ⬚

Leisure facilities: 🎣 ⊕ ➤ ⌐ ∪
Main A96 Inverness-Aberdeen road, on right, 1 ml from Nairn.

Key to symbols
is on back flap

VAT is shown at 17.5%: changes in this rate may affect prices.

NAIRN, Map Ref. 4C8

Nairn Lochloy Holiday Park

East Beach, Nairn IV12 4PH. Tel: (01667) 453764

Thistle Commended accommodation. Magnificent safe, sandy beach next to the park. Super seaside holiday town of Nairn within easy walking distance. Amusement arcade, launderette, children's play area. Tourers welcome. Riverside and woodland walks. Wide choice of restaurants, pubs and take-aways within easy walking distance.

Prices: £80-£385 per week.
Contact Parkdean Holidays (0191) 2240500 Brochure.

Quote Ref. STB

| ✓ | ✓ | ✓ | ✓ |

258

Nairn Lochloy Holiday Park, East Beach, Nairn, IV12 4PH
☎ *(Nairn) 01667 453764 Fax: 01667 455437*
Booking Enquiries: Parkdean Holidays Ltd, Cragside House, 42a Heaton Road, Newcastle upon Tyne
☎ *0191 224 0500, Fax: 0191 224 0490*
6¹/₂ acres, grassy, sandy, mid Mar-Oct, prior booking in peak periods, latest time of arrival 2200, overnight holding area. Extra charge for electricity, awnings.

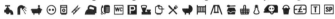

75 tourers £6.00-10.50 or 75 motors £6.00-10.50 or 25 tents £5.50-7.50.
Total Touring Pitches 100.
88 Holiday Caravans to let, sleep 4-8 £95.00-400.00, total sleeping capacity 268, min. let 2 nights.

Leisure facilities: ● ☉ ▶ ⚲ ∪ ⬤
From either Inverness or Aberdeen take A96. East Beach in town of Nairn adjacent Dunbar Golf course.

BY NAIRN, Map Ref. 4C8

40

Spindrift Caravan Park, Little Kildrummie, by Nairn, Inverness-shire, IV12 5QU
☎ *(Nairn) 01667 453992*
Booking Enquiries: Mr Guillot
3 acres, grassy, sandy, level, Apr-Oct, prior booking in peak periods, latest time of arrival 2200. Extra charge for electricity.

40 tourers £5.50-7.50 or 40 motors £5.50-7.50 or 40 tents £5.50-7.50.
Total Touring Pitches 40.
Leisure facilities: ▶ ⚲ ⚲ ∪ ⬤ ✚ ⬤ ⚡
From Nairn take B9090 S, Nairn/Cawdor road, for 1¹/₂ mls. Turn right at sharp left hand bend onto unclassified road. Site entrance 400 yds on left.

TELEPHONE DIALLING CODES

On 16 April 1995 all UK area codes starting **0** will start **01**.
From August 1994 until 16 April 1995, the new codes will be run in parallel with the old ones.
If you experience difficulty in connecting a call, please call Directory Enquiries – **192** – for advice. Please note: A charge will be made for this service when using a private phone.

BY NAIRN, Map Ref. 4C8

Laikenbuie Holidays
Grantown Road, Nairn IV12 5QN   Tel: (01667) 454630

Watch Roe deer, perhaps Osprey fishing. Beautiful outlook over natural woods and lake. Two modern 2/3 bedroom 34' caravans, four miles south of Nairn. On croft with sheep, free range hens, organic garden, trout fishing. Central to beaches, Cairngorms, Loch Ness. **Colour brochure. No smoking.**

INSPECTED

Booking Enquiries: Mrs Therese Muskus, Laikenbuie Holidays, Grantown Road, Nairn, IV12 5QN
☎ *(Nairn)* 01667 454630
2 Holiday Caravans to let, sleep 6 £90.00-260.00, total sleeping capacity 12, min. let weekend, Mar-Nov.

Leisure facilities:
4 miles S of Nairn on A939

NEWTONMORE, Inverness-shire, Map Ref. 4B11

75

Invernahavon Caravan Park, Glentruim Estate, Newtonmore, Inverness-shire, PH20 1BE
☎ *(Newtonmore)* 01540 673534/673219
12½ acres, grassy, level, Mar-Oct, latest time of arrival 2200, overnight holding area. Extra charge for electricity, showers.

35 tourers £6.00-7.00 or 25 motors £6.00-7.00 or 25 tents £5.00-6.00.
Total Touring Pitches 75.
Leisure facilities:
Situated 500 mtrs off A9 trunk road, 8 mls N of Dalwhinnie and 3 mls S of Newtonmore.

NEWTON STEWART, Wigtownshire, Map Ref. 1H10

86

Creebridge Caravan Park, Newton Stewart, Wigtownshire, DG8 6AJ
☎ *(Newton Stewart)* 01671 402324
4½ acres, mixed, Mar-Oct, prior booking in peak periods, latest time of arrival 2000, overnight holding area. Extra charge for electricity, awnings.

15 tourers £6.70-9.00 or 5 motors £6.50-8.50 or 20 tents £6.00-8.00.
Total Touring Pitches 45.
5 Holiday Caravans to let, sleep 6 £125.00-200.00, total sleeping capacity 30, min. let 1 night.

Leisure facilities:
¼ ml E of Newton Stewart off A75, or through centre of Newton Stewart over bridge to Minnigaff, 300 mtrs on right.

Key to symbols is on back flap

VAT is shown at 17.5%: changes in this rate may affect prices.

NEWTON STEWART, Wigtownshire, Map Ref. 1H10

145

Three Lochs Holiday Park, Kirkcowan, Wigtownshire, DG8 0EP
☎ *(Kirkcowan) 01671 830304*
25 acres, mixed, Easter-Oct, latest time of arrival 2100, overnight holding area.
Extra charge for electricity.

🛁 🍴 ➡ ☉ ▯ ⚡ 🚿 ▯ E 🆆 🅿 🕁 ✕ 🐕 ➡ ▥ ⚠ ♨ ▯ 🦽 🚙 ☎ SP

85 tourers £7.00-8.50 or 85 motors £7.00-8.50 or 85 tents £7.00-8.50.
Total Touring Pitches 45.
8 Holiday Caravans to let, sleep 4-6 £105.00-230.00, total sleeping capacity 48,
min. let 2 nights.

🛁 🍴 ➡ ☉ 🚐 ▯ E 🆆 🅿 🕁 ✕ 🐕 ➡ ▥ ⚠ 🦽 🚙 ▱

Leisure facilities: 🎣 🎯 ⛳ ▶ 🏌 🏊 U ✓ 🎾

From Newton Stewart take A75 west for 7 mls (ignore B735). Site signposted on right.
From Stranraer, A75 to Glenluce. Left at top of village. Follow signs for Whitecairn Farm.
Site 4 mls beyond farm.

NORTH BERWICK, East Lothian, Map Ref. 2E4

North Berwick Tantallon Rhodes Caravan Park
Easy access to beach and Glen golf course. East Lothian
offers golfing galore, beautiful beaches, shops, castles,
museums, something for everyone.
Holiday homes for hire and sale.
Touring and tenting pitches price £5.50 to £9.50.
Fax or phone 01620 893348   Dept. STB C&C
Lime Grove, North Berwick, East Lothian.

218

Tantallon Rhodes Caravan Park, Lime Grove, North Berwick, East Lothian, EH39 5NJ
☎ *(North Berwick) 01620 893348 Fax: 01620 893348*
10 acres, grassy, stony, end Mar-end Oct, prior booking in peak periods, latest time
of arrival 2000, overnight holding area. Extra charge for electricity, awnings.

🛁 🍴 ☉ ▯ ⚡ 🚿 🚐 ▯ E 🆆 🅿 🛒 🕁 ✕ 🐕 ⚠ 🦽 🚙 ☎ 🌳 🎾 ▱ T SP

200 tourers £5.50-9.50 or 200 motors £5.50-9.50 or 200 tents £5.00-9.50.
Total Touring Pitches 200.
5 Holiday Caravans to let, sleep 6 £100.00-325.00, total sleeping capacity 30,
min. let 3 nights.

🛁 🍴 ☉ ▯ E 🆆 🅿 🛒 🕁 ✕ 🐕 ⚠ 🚙 🦽 ▯ 🚾 🎾 ▱ T

Leisure facilities: ▶

Located on E side of North Berwick between town and Tantallon Castle
and just off A198 Dunbar road.

NORTH KESSOCK, Ross-shire, Map Ref. 4B8

Coulmore Bay Caravan Park
Booking Enquiries: Mrs B Warne, Kimberley Holiday Homes, Nethy Bridge,
Inverness-shire, PH25 3DB
☎ *(Nethybridge) 01479 821476*
2 Holiday Caravans to let, sleep 2-6 £150.00-195.00,
total sleeping capacity 10, Apr-Oct.

🛁 🍴 ▯ E 🆆 🅿 🛒 ✕ 🐕 🚙 ◎ 🦽 ▯ 🚾

From Inverness take A9 over Kessock Brdg turn 1st left to North Kessock.
Turn right at start of village, continue 1 1/2 mls on shore road.

OBAN, Argyll, Map Ref. 1E2

240

North Ledaig Caravan Park, Connel, by Oban, Argyll, PA37 1RT
☎ *(Connel) 0163171 291 Fax: 0163171 291*
28 acres, grassy, hard-standing, Easter-Oct, prior booking in peak periods,
latest time of arrival 2000, overnight holding area, restricted to 120 pitches for
Caravan Club. Extra charge for electricity.

🔥 📶 ☉ 🗑 ⚡ 🚗 🏪 E WC P ⚡ ☇ ✗ 🐕 ♨ ⛟ 🐟 🎣 🦜 D

240 tourers £6.30-10.00 or 240 motors £6.30-10.00. Total Touring Pitches 240.
No tents.
Leisure facilities: ⛵ 🦆 ⚓
Site is situated on A828, Oban-Fort William, approx. 1 ml N of Connel Bridge.

OBAN CARAVAN & CAMPING
Gallanachmore Farm, Oban, Argyll PA34 4QH
Telephone: (01631) 62425
In an area of outstanding scenic beauty, Gallanachmore Farm is situated
on the seafront overlooking the Island of Kerrera. The Park provides
excellent toilet and shower facilities, a well-stocked shop/off-license,
launderette, children's play area and lends itself superbly for boating,
fishing and scuba diving. Pets welcome.

150

**Oban Caravan & Camping Park, Gallanachmore Farm, Gallanach Road,
Oban, Argyll, PA34 4QH**
☎ *(Oban) 01631 62425 Fax: 01631 66624*
Booking Enquiries: Brian & Sylvia Thompson
15 acres, grassy, hard-standing, level, Apr-mid Oct.
Extra charge for electricity, awnings.

🔥 📶 ☉ 🗑 ⚡ 🚗 🏪 E WC P ☇ ✗ 🐕 ♨ ⛟ 🦜 🐟 🎣

30 tourers £5.50-6.50 and 20 motors £5.50-6.50 and 150 tents £5.50-6.50.
Total Touring Pitches 200.
10 Holiday Caravans to let, sleep 6 £130.00-250.00, total sleeping capacity 60,
min. let weekend (low season).

🔥 📶 ☉ 🚗 🖵 E WC P ☇ ✗ 🐕 ♨ ⛟ 🖉 🗑 🔥 † 🎣

Leisure facilities: ⚓ ▶ ⛵ 🚣 ∪ ⚓ 🦆 🎿
2 mls S of Oban on coast road from town centre. Follow signs to Gallanach.

50

Oban Divers Caravan Park, Glenshellach Road, Oban, Argyll, PA34 4QH
☎ *(Oban) 01631 62755 Fax: 01631 62755*
4 acres, mixed, Mar-Nov, prior booking in peak periods, latest time of arrival 1800,
overnight holding area. Extra charge for electricity, awnings, showers.

🔥 📶 ☉ ⚡ 🚗 🏪 E WC P ⚡ ☇ ✗ ♨ ⛟ 🐟 🎣 🦜 D

21 tourers £6.50-7.50 or 21 motors £6.50-7.50 or 31 tents £5.00-8.00.
Total Touring Pitches 50.
Leisure facilities: ∪ 🦆
Take A85 into Oban, turn right up High Street. Leaving Tourist Office in right
take first left up Glenshellach Road for 1½ mls. Park on left.

Key to symbols
is on back flap

VAT is shown at 17.5%: changes in this rate may affect prices.

ONICH – PALNACKIE, by Castle Douglas

ONICH, by Fort William Inverness-shire, Map Ref. 1F1

Corran Caravans, Moss Cottage, Onich, by Fort William, Inverness-shire, PH33 6SE
☎ (Onich) 018553 208 Fax: 01397 700133
1¹/₂ acres, grassy, hard-standing, Jan-Dec, prior booking in peak periods.
Extra charge for electricity, awnings.

10 tourers £6.00-7.00 or 4 motors £6.00-7.00 or 5 tents £6.00-7.00.
Total Touring Pitches 14.
10 Holiday Caravans to let, sleep 6 £100.00-250.00, total sleeping capacity 60,
min. let 1 night.

Leisure facilities: ▶ ∪ ♣ ⚓
4 mls from Ballachulish Bridge and ¹/₂ ml through Onich village, turn left,
down road to end, turn right uphill to Moss Cottage.

OXTON, by Lauder Berwickshire, Map Ref. 2E6

Carfraemill Chalet & Caravan Park, Carfraemill, Oxton, by Lauder, TD2 6RD
☎ (Oxton) 01578 750215
10 acres, grassy, hard-standing, level, Apr-Oct, prior booking in peak periods.
Extra charge for electricity, awnings.

30 tourers £6.00-7.50 or 30 motors £6.00-7.50 or 15 tents £5.00-6.00.
Total Touring Pitches 45.
Leisure facilities: ▶ ♪ ∪
Site near Carfraemill Hotel, on junc A697-A68, 21 mls S of Edinburgh.

PALNACKIE, by Castle Douglas Kirkcudbrightshire, Map Ref. 2B10

Barlochan Caravan Park, Palnackie, by Castle Douglas, Kirkcudbrightshire, DG7 1PF
☎ (Palnackie) 0155660 256
Booking Enquiries: Barlochan Caravan Park, c/o Booking Office, Brighouse Bay,
Borgue, Kirkcudbrightshire, DG6 4TS
☎ (Borgue) 015577 267
8 acres, mixed, Apr-Oct, prior booking in peak periods, latest time of arrival 2130,
overnight holding area. Extra charge for electricity, awnings.

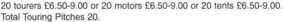

20 tourers £6.50-9.00 or 20 motors £6.50-9.00 or 20 tents £6.50-9.00.
Total Touring Pitches 20.
9 Holiday Caravans to let, sleep 4-8 £95.00-240.00, total sleeping capacity 56,
min. let 2 nights.

Leisure facilities: ⟜ ⚓ ▶ ♪ ⚓ ∪ ♦ ✦ ⚓
From Dalbeattie take A711 W turning left at junction in ¹/₂ ml signposted Palnackie.
Park on right in 2 mls.

PARTON, Kirkcudbrightshire, Map Ref. 2A10

LOCH KEN HOLIDAY PARK
Parton, Castle Douglas DG7 3NE
Telephone: (01644) 470282   Fax: (01644) 470297
On the shores of the loch in an area of outstanding natural beauty, this park is renowned for friendliness and cleanliness. Superb Thistle Commended caravans for hire. The touring caravan and tent pitches also overlook the loch. Ideal base for exploring Galloway. Many water and land-based activities nearby. 7 miles from Castle Douglas A713.

Holiday caravans from £135 per week.
Touring caravans and family tents
from £6.50 per night.

Loch Ken Holiday Park, Parton, Castle Douglas, Kirkcudbrightshire, DG7 3NE
☎ *(Parton) 01644 470282 Fax: 01644 470297*
7 acres, mixed, late Mar-early Nov, prior booking in peak periods,
latest time of arrival 2000. Extra charge for electricity, awnings, showers.

80 tourers from £6.50 or 80 motors from £6.50 or 80 tents from £6.00.
Total Touring Pitches 80.
14 Holiday Caravans to let, sleep 6 £140.00-325.00, total sleeping capacity 84,
min. let 2 nights.

Leisure facilities:
A713 7 mls from Castle Douglas and ½ ml N of Parton.

PEEBLES, Map Ref. 2C6

Crossburn Caravan Park, Edinburgh Road, Peebles, EH45 8ED
☎ *(Peebles) 01721 720501 Fax: 01721 720501*
6 acres, mixed, Apr-mid Oct, prior booking in peak periods, latest time of arrival 2300,
overnight holding area. Extra charge for electricity, awnings.

35 tourers from £8.10 or 35 motors from £7.40 or 35 tents from £7.75.
Total Touring Pitches 35.
4 Holiday Caravans to let, sleep 3-5 from £150.00, total sleeping capacity 18,
min. let 2 nights.

Leisure facilities:
½ ml N of Peebles on A703.

Scotland for Golf . . .
Find out more about golf in Scotland. There's more to it than just the championship courses so get in touch with us now for information on the hidden gems of Scotland.
Write to: **Information Unit, Scottish Tourist Board,**
23 Ravelston Terrace, Edinburgh EH4 3EU
or call: 0131-332 2433

VAT is shown at 17.5%: changes in this rate may affect prices.

PEEBLES, Map Ref. 2C6

ROSETTA CARAVAN PARK
Rosetta Road, Peebles EH45 8PG   **Tel: (01721) 720770**

A family owned, mature country park of 27 acres, within 10 minutes walking distance of Peebles High Street. Adjacent to 18-hole golf course. Amenities include bowling green, putting green, children's games facilities, licensed lounge bar.

Winner of Calor Award 1990-91 Best Park in Scotland.
Also finalists in 1994.

Rosetta Caravan & Camping Park, Rosetta Road, Peebles, EH45 8PG
☎ *(Peebles) 01721 720770*
24 acres, grassy, Apr-Oct, latest time of arrival 2300, overnight holding area. Extra charge for electricity, awnings.

🔥 👜 ☺ ⊡ ✒ 🛢 🎮 ⛺ E 🚾 P 🛒 ♻ ✗ 🐎 🏛 ⚠ 🍴 🎒 ♨ 🛢 😊 🍼

100 tourers £7.50-8.00 or 100 motors £7.50-8.00 or 30 tents £6.30-7.00. Total Touring Pitches 130.
Leisure facilities: ● ✪ ▶ ✦ ∪
Travelling W from centre of Peebles on A72 towards Glasgow turn right in town onto unclassified road signposted Rosetta. Site ¹/₂ ml on left.

PENINVER, by Campbeltown, Argyll, Map Ref. 1E7

Peninver Sands Caravan Park, Craigview, Campbeltown, Argyll, PA28
☎ *(Campbeltown) 01586 552262*
2³/₄ acres, mixed, Apr-Oct, latest time of arrival 2100.
Extra charge for electricity, awnings.

🔥 👜 ☺ ⊡ ✒ 🛢 🎮 E 🚾 P ♻ ✗ 🐎 ⚠ 🛢 😊 🍼 SP

6 tourers from £4.00 or 6 motors from £4.00. Total Touring Pitches 6. No tents.
6 Holiday Caravans to let, sleep 6 £100.00-200.00, total sleeping capacity 36, min. let 2 nights.

🔥 👜 ☺ 🎮 E 🚾 P ♻ ✗ 🐎 ⚠ 🗄 ✏ 🖥 ♨

Leisure facilities: ✦
From Campbeltown take B842 N for 4¹/₂ mls. Site on right as you enter Peninver.

PERTH, Map Ref. 2C2

Cleeve Caravan Park, Glasgow Road, Perth, PH2 0PH
☎ *(Perth) 01738 39521/639521*
Booking Enquiries: Perth & Kinross District Council, 3 High Street, Perth, PH1 5PH
☎ *(Perth) 01738 39911 ext 3603/3605 (Nov-Mar)*
5¹/₃ acres, mixed, Apr-Oct, prior booking in peak periods, latest time of arrival 2100, overnight holding area. Extra charge for electricity, awnings.

🔥 👜 ☺ ⊡ ✒ 🛢 🎮 E 🚾 P 🛒 ♻ ✗ 🐎 ⚠ 🛢 😊 🍼 D

100 tourers £7.00-8.20 or 100 motors £7.00-8.20 or 18 tents £6.40. Total Touring Pitches 100.
On Glasgow Road, Perth approx. 350 mtrs E of A9/Perth by-pass intersection.

PETERSPORT, Isle of Benbecula, Western Isles, Map Ref. 3A9

Booking Enquiries: Mrs M Bagley, 3 Grimsay Island, Petersport, Benbecula, Western Isles
☎ *(Benbecula) 01870 602473*
Holiday Caravan to let, sleeps 4-6 £65.00-100.00, Mar-Oct.

🛆 🛝 🖭 🖵 E 🅆 🅿 ⅃ ⅄ ✕ 🐴 🛶 🎮 ⚠ 🏕 ⌀ 🖥 🔥 ⚒

Leisure facilities: 🎣
On B891 Grimsay/Petersport road.

PITLOCHRY, Perthshire, Map Ref. 2B1

315

Faskally Caravan Park, Pitlochry, Perthshire, PH16 5LA
☎ *(Pitlochry) 01796 472007 Fax: 01796 473896*
23 acres, grassy, level, sloping, sheltered, mid Mar-Oct, latest time of arrival 2300.
Extra charge for electricity, awnings.

🛆 🛝 🛶 ☉ 🖥 ✐ 🖭 🗟 🅆 🅿 ♂ ✕ 🐴 🎮 ⚠ 🍷 🆁 ⚖ ♨ ♪ 🦮 🐕 £

255 tourers £8.50-9.50 or 255 motors £8.20-9.20 or 100 tents £7.60-8.60.
Total Touring Pitches 255.
40 Holiday Caravans to let, sleep 6 £200.00-360.00, total sleeping capacity 240, min. let weekend.

🛆 🛝 🛶 ☉ 🖵 E 🅆 🅿 🐴 🎮 ⚠ ⌀ 🖥 🔥 £ 🄳

Leisure facilities: 🏊 ⛳ 🎣 🔍
Two mls N of Pitlochry on B8019 to Killiecrankie.

MILTON OF FONAB CARAVAN SITE
Pitlochry, Perthshire PH16 5NA
Telephone: (01796) 472882 Fax: (01796) 474363
Milton of Fonab – a quiet site that lies on the banks of
the River Tummel ¹/₂ mile south of Pitlochry.
Static caravans for hire, touring pitches available.
Showers, baths, laundry facilities and a shop on site.

210

Milton of Fonab Caravan Park, Pitlochry, Perthshire, PH16 5NA
☎ *(Pitlochry) 01796 472882 Fax: 01796 474363*
16 acres, grassy, level, sheltered, Mar-Oct, prior booking in peak periods,
latest time of arrival 2100. Extra charge for electricity, awnings, showers.

🛆 🛝 🛶 ☉ 🖥 ✐ 🖭 E 🅆 🅿 ⅃ ♂ ✕ 🐴 🎮 ⚖ ♨ 🦮 🐕

154 tourers £8.00-8.50 or 154 motors £7.50-8.00 or 154 tents £8.00-8.50.
Total Touring Pitches 154.
36 Holiday Caravans to let, sleep 6 £160.00-310.00, total sleeping capacity 216, min. let 2 nights.

🛆 🛝 🛝 ☉ 🖭 🖵 E 🅆 🅿 ⅃ ♂ ✕ 🐴 🎮 🏕 ⌀ 🖥 🔥 🄳

Leisure facilities: 🎣
From S take Pitlochry filter road. Site is ¹/₂ ml S of Pitlochry.

Key to symbols
is on back flap

BY PITLOCHRY, Perthshire, Map Ref. 2B1

Dalshian
Booking Enquiries: Mr Peter Telford, Dalshian House, Old Perth Road, Pitlochry, Perthshire, PH16 5JS
☎ *(Pitlochry) 01796 472173*
7 Holiday Caravans to let, sleep 6 £160.00-240.00, total sleeping capacity 42, min. let weekend, Apr-Oct.

Travelling from S take slip road off A9 to Pitlochry.
Then take first turn on right at signpost marked Dalshian.

PITTENWEEM, Fife, Map Ref. 2E3

Grangemuir Woodland Park Caravan Site, Grangemuir, Pittenweem, Fife, KY10 2RB
☎ *(Anstruther) 01333 311213*
6 acres, mixed, Apr-Oct, latest time of arrival 2200, overnight holding area.
Extra charge for electricity, awnings.

45 tourers £7.50-8.00 or 45 motors £7.00-7.50 or 45 tents £6.00-7.00.
Total Touring Pitches 45.
Leisure facilities:
Approach by B9171 from N. Sign Grangemuir.

POOLEWE, Ross-shire, Map Ref. 3F7

Camping and Caravanning Club Site, Inverewe Gardens, Poolewe, Ross-shire, IV22 2LE
☎ *(Poolewe) 01445 86249/781249*
Booking Enquiries: Camping and Caravanning Club Ltd, Greenfields House, Westwood Way, Coventry, CV4 8JH
☎ *(Coventry) 01203 694995 Fax: 01203 694886*
4 acres, mixed, Mar-Sep, prior booking in peak periods, latest time of arrival 2100.
Extra charge for electricity.

50 tourers £5.72-6.40 or 50 motors £5.72-6.40 or 50 tents £5.72-6.40.
Total Touring Pitches 50.
Leisure facilities:
By the BP filling station in village of Poolewe.

PORT ELLEN, Map Ref. 1C6

Booking Enquiries: Mrs Whyte, Glenmachrie, Port Ellen, Isle of Islay, Argyll
☎ *(Port Ellen) 01496 302560*
Holiday Caravan to let, sleeps 6 £150.00-200.00, min.let weekend, Jan-Dec.

Leisure facilities:
From Port Ellen take A846 for 4 mls to Glenmachrie Farm.

PORTPATRICK, Wigtownshire, Map Ref. 1F11

Galloway Point Holiday Park, Portpatrick, Wigtownshire, DG9 9AA
☎ *(Portpatrick) 01776 810561 Fax: 01776 810561*
19 acres, mixed, Mar-Oct, prior booking in peak periods, latest time of arrival 2200, overnight holding area. Extra charge for electricity.

🔥 🖈 ➡ ⊙ 🗑 ✚ 🚙 🎪 ⌷ E 🚾 P 🅿 ♻ ✕ 🐕 🏛 ⚠ 🍴 🍽 🛎 ♨ 🔌 ☎

40 tourers £10.00-12.00 or 10 motors £10.00-12.00 or 60 tents £8.00-12.00.
Total Touring Pitches 100.
5 Holiday Caravans to let, sleep 6 £175.00-275.00, total sleeping capacity 30, min.let 4 nights.

🍴 ♻ ✕ 🏛 ⚠ ⌀ 🗑 ♨

Leisure facilities: ⏰ 🏌 ⛵ ⛳ 🏊 ⛵
Take A75 N from Dumfries, A77 to Portpatrick, or take A77 S from Glasgow. On entering Portpatrick take first left. Site is ¼ ml on right.

Sunnymeade Caravan Park, Portpatrick, Wigtownshire, DG9 8LN
☎ *(Portpatrick) 01671 810293*
8 acres, grassy, hard-standing, level, Mar-Oct, prior booking in peak periods. Extra charge for electricity, showers.

🔥 🖈 ⊙ 🗑 ✚ 🚙 🎪 E 🚾 P 🅿 ♻ ✕ 🐕 🛎 ♨ ☎

15 tourers £6.00-8.50 or 15 motors £6.00-8.50 or 15 tents £6.00-8.50.
Total Touring Pitches 15.
5 Holiday Caravans to let, sleep 6 £110.00-250.00, total sleeping capacity 30, min. let 2 nights.

Ⓜ 🔥 🖈 ⊙ 🚙 ⌷ E 🚾 P 🅿 ♻ ✕ 🐕 ⌀ 🗑 ♨

Leisure facilities: ✪ 🏌 ⛵ ⛳ 🏊 ⛵
Take A77 to Portpatrick, on entering the village turn left. Park ¼ ml on left.

PORTREE, Isle of Skye, Inverness-shire,, Map Ref. 3D9

Torvaig Caravan & Camping Site, Portree, Isle of Skye, Inverness-shire, IV51 9HS
☎ *(Portree) 01478 2209/612209*
3 acres, grassy, hard-standing, Apr-Oct, latest time of arrival 2200.
Extra charge for awnings.

🔥 🖈 ⊙ 🗑 🎪 🚾 P 🅿 ✕ 🐕 🛎 ♨ ☎

30 tourers £6.00 and 30 motors £6.00 and 100 tents £6.00.
Total Touring Pitches 160.
1 ml N of Portree on A855 Staffin main road.

PORTSONACHAN, Argyll, Map Ref. 1F3

Booking Enquiries: Mr & Mrs J C Soar, Sonachan House, Portsonachan, by Dalmally, Argyll, PA33 1BN
☎ *(Kilchrenan) 018663 240 Fax: 018663 241*
4 Holiday Caravans to let, sleep 6 £105.00-260.00, total sleeping capacity 24, min. let 2 nights, Apr-Oct.

Ⓜ 🔥 🖈 ⊙ 🚙 ⌷ E 🚾 P 🅿 ♻ ✕ 🐕 ➡ 🏛 ⚠ 🚪 ◎ 🗑 ♨ 🎣 🇹

Leisure facilities: 🎣 ✪ 🏌 ⛵ ⛳ 🏊 ⛳ 🗺 ⛷ ⛵ 🏹 ⛸ 🎿
On B840 SE Loch Awe side. 4½ mls from Cladich road junction.

Key to symbols
is on back flap

RESIPOLE, by Acharacle, Argyll, Map Ref. 1D1

RESIPOLE CARAVAN AND CAMPING PARK
Loch Sunart, Acharacle, Argyll PH36 4HX
Telephone: (01967) 431617/431235   Fax: (01967) 431777
On the unspoiled Ardnamurchan peninsula, this spacious, well managed park offers fine views and modern, well maintained facilities. These include: shop, games room, laundry, drying room and slipway. Close by an excellent restaurant and bar. Ideal centre for touring, fishing and hill walking in an area of outstanding beauty.

Resipole Caravan Park, Resipole, by Acharacle, Argyll
☎ *(Salen) 01967431 235/617 Fax: 01967431 777*
5 acres, grassy, level, Easter-Oct, latest time of arrival 2300.
Extra charge for electricity.

30 tourers £6.50-7.50 and 5 motors £6.50-7.50 and 10 tents £6.50-7.50.
Total Touring Pitches 45.
8 Holiday Caravans to let, sleep 2-5 £155.00-220.00, total sleeping capacity 36, min. let 3 nights (low season).

Leisure facilities: 🎣 ⛵ 🅺
Take A861 from Corran Ferry. Site is 7½ mls from Strontian on the Salen road.

ROCKCLIFFE, by Dalbeattie, Kirkcudbrightshire, Map Ref. 2B10

Castle Point Caravan Park, Barcloy Road, Rockcliffe, by Dalbeattie, Kirkcudbrightshire, DG5 4QL
☎ *(Rockcliffe) 01556 630248*
Booking Enquiries: 34 Southfields (before April), East Molesey, Surrey, KT8 0BP
☎ *0181 398 1289*
3 acres, grassy, level, sloping, Mar-Oct, prior booking in peak periods.
Extra charge for electricity, awnings.

22 tourers £6.50-8.50 or 22 motors £6.50-8.50 or 22 tents £6.50-8.50.
Total Touring Pitches 22.
5 Holiday Caravans to let, sleep 6 £110.00-240.00, total sleeping capacity 30, min. let 1 night.

From Dalbeattie take A710 SW for 5 mls, turn right to Rockcliffe, then after 1 ml turn left down signposted road to Site.

GRADING
YOUR GUARANTEE
OF QUALITY

Important: Prices stated are estimates and may be subject to amendments

ROSEMARKIE, Ross-shire, Map Ref. 4B8

Camping & Caravanning Club Site, Rosemarkie, Fortrose, Ross-shire, IV10 8UW
☎ *(Fortrose) 01381 621117*
Booking Enquiries: The Camping & Caravanning Club, Greenfields House,
Westwood Way, Coventry, CV4 8JH
☎ *(Coventry) 01203 694995 (out of season) Fax: 01203 694886 (out of season)*
5 acres, grassy, stony, level, Mar-Sep, prior booking in peak periods, latest time of
arrival 2100. Extra charge for electricity.

60 tourers £5.72-6.40 or 60 motors £5.72-6.40 or 60 tents £5.72-6.40.
Total Touring Pitches 60.
Follow A9 over Kessock Bridge. Turn right at Tore roundabout on A832 signposted
Fortrose and Cromarty. In Fortrose turn right. opp. police houses down to coastroad.

ROSLIN, Midlothian, Map Ref. 2D5

Slatebarns Caravan Park, Slatebarns Farm, Roslin, Midlothian, EH25 9PU
☎ 0131 440 2192
2½ acres, mixed, Easter-Oct, prior booking in peak periods, latest time of arrival
2200, overnight holding area. Extra charge for electricity, awnings.

30 tourers from £7.00 or 30 motors from £7.00. Total Touring Pitches 30. No tents.
From city by-pass turn off at Straiton junct. for Peebles. Turn off at Bilston onto
B7006 signed Roslin. Follow Roslin Chapel signs. Site 100yds beyond Chapel.

ROSNEATH, by Helensburgh, Dunbartonshire, Map Ref. 1G4

Rosneath Castle Caravan Park, Rosneath, by Helensburgh,
Dunbartonshire, G84 0QS
☎ *(Clynder) 01436 831208 Fax: 01436 831978*
55 acres, sandy, hard-standing, level, Apr-Oct, prior booking in peak periods, latest
time of arrival 1800, overnight holding area. Extra charge for electricity, showers.

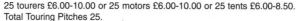

25 tourers £6.00-10.00 or 25 motors £6.00-10.00 or 25 tents £6.00-8.50.
Total Touring Pitches 25.
12 Holiday Caravans to let, sleep 6-8 £120.00-345.00, total sleeping capacity 82,
min. let 2 nights.

Leisure facilities:
Take B833 from Garelochhead through Clynder and Rosneath villages.

WELCOME

Whenever you are in Scotland, you can be sure of a warm welcome at your
nearest Tourist Information Centre.
For guide books, maps, souvenirs, our Centres provide a service second to
none – many now offer bureau-de-change facilities. And, of course, Tourist
Information Centres offer free, expert advice on what to see and do, route-
planning and accommodation for everyone – visitors and residents alike!

Key to symbols
is on back flap

ROUNDYHILL, by Glamis, Angus, Map Ref. 2D1

DRUMSHADEMUIR CARAVAN PARK
Roundyhill, by Glamis, Forfar, Angus DD8 1QT
Telephone: (01575) 573284

Calor Award 1994. Family run, situated in the Strathmore Valley overlooking the Sidlaw Hills. 2 miles north of the historic village of Glamis and 2 miles south of Kirriemuir. The Angus glens are five miles north which are ideal for hill-walking, fishing, pony-trekking. Park tavern serving evening meals, lunches daily.

113

Drumshademuir Caravan Park, Roundyhill, by Glamis, Angus, DD8 1QT
☎ *(Kirriemuir)* 01575 573284
7½ acres, grassy, hard-standing, level, mid Mar-Oct, prior booking in peak periods, latest time of arrival 2300, overnight holding area. Extra charge for electricity, awnings.

🕭 🏕 ⛟ ⊙ 📷 ⚡ 🚗 ⚐ E ᵂᶜ 🅿 ♨ ♁ ✕ ⛺ 🏵 ⚠ ❗ Ⓡ 🍴 ⛓ ♨ 🔌 🔆 ☎ Ⓓ

80 tourers £7.00-7.50 or 80 motors £7.00-7.50 or 80 tents £5.25-5.50.
Total Touring Pitches 80.
Leisure facilities: ✪
From Perth take A94 to Aberdeen, turn left. Glamis A928. Site 2½ mls on right.

ROWARDENNAN, Stirlingshire, Map Ref. 1G4

200

Cashel Campsite, Forestry Commission, Rowardennan, Stirlingshire, G63 0AW
☎ *(Balmaha)* 0136087 234/018772 383
Booking Enquiries: Forestry Commission, Aberfoyle, Perthshire, FK8 3UX
☎ *(Aberfoyle)* 018772 383 *Fax: 018772 694*
12 acres, grassy, sandy, stony, Apr-Oct, prior booking in peak periods, latest time of arrival 2200, overnight holding area. Extra charge for electricity, awnings, showers.

🕭 🏕 ⊙ 📷 ⚡ ⚐ E ᵂᶜ 🅿 ⛺ ⚠ 🔌 🔆 ☎ ⊞ Ⓓ

135 tourers £6.00-7.50 or 135 motors £6.00-7.50 or 135 tents £6.00-7.50.
Total Touring Pitches 135.
From Drymen take B837 Drymen/Balmaha/ Rowardennan road.
Site lies 3 mls NW of Balmaha.

TELEPHONE DIALLING CODES

On 16 April 1995 all UK area codes starting **0** will start **01**.

From August 1994 until 16 April 1995, the new codes will be run in parallel with the old ones.
If you experience difficulty in connecting a call, please call Directory Enquiries – **192** – for advice. Please note: A charge will be made for this service when using a private phone.

ST ANDREWS, Fife, Map Ref. 2E3

Craigtoun Meadows
Mount Melville, St Andrews, Fife KY16 8PQ
Tel: (01334) 475959   Fax: (01334) 476424

One of Scotland's best known and highest classified and graded Caravan Holiday Parks. Winner of the Calor Gas "Best Park in Scotland" Award, 1989, 1994. AA 5 Pennants and AA winner of "Best Scottish Park" in 1984 and 1990/1991. "Excellent" Graded. Special attention has been paid to landscaping and the Park is a most attractive place to be at all times of year. Besides good indoor and outdoor games facilities the Park has a tennis court and mini-gym. Also a launderette, licensed shop and restaurant. The 32 Caravan Holiday Homes for letting are all Thistle Commended. All 100 Touring/Tenting pitches have water-points, electric hook-ups and waste gullies and several of these have been upgraded to patio pitches with Summerhouses and Screening.
Special prices during British Golf Open in July.

Free Brochure. **Telephoning Answering Service. Credit Card Booking**   *(Ref: STB C&C 95)*

Craigtoun Meadows Holiday Park, Mount Melville, St Andrews, Fife, KY16 8PQ
☎ *(St Andrews) 01334 475959 Fax: 01334 476424*
37 acres, mixed, Mar-Oct, prior booking in peak periods, latest time of arrival 2100, overnight holding area. Extra charge for awnings.

241

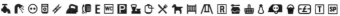

100 tourers £10.75-11.75 or 100 motors £10.75-11.75 or 100 tents £10.75-11.75. Total Touring Pitches 100.
36 Holiday Caravans to let, sleep 4-6 £120.00-330.00, total sleeping capacity 214, min. let 3 days (low season).

Leisure facilities: ♦ ⊕ ✗ ℺
From M90 (Jct 8) take A91 to St Andrews turn right 400 yds after Guardbridge, signposted Strathkinness. Turn left at second crossroads after Strathkinness.

Mr & Mrs C Kennedy, Clayton Caravan Park, St Andrews, Fife, KY16 9YE
☎ *(Balmullo) 01334 870242/870630*
40 acres, mixed, Mar-Oct, prior booking in peak periods, latest time of arrival 2300, overnight holding area. Extra charge for electricity, showers.

276

26 tourers £9.00-10.50 or 26 motors £8.00-9.50 or 26 tents £6.00-10.50. Total Touring Pitches 26.
Leisure facilities: ♦ ⊕ ► U
4½ mls W of St Andrews on A91, between Dairsie and Guardbridge.

Kinkell Braes Caravan Park, Abbeyford Caravans, St Andrews, Fife, KY16 8PX
☎ *(St Andrews) 01334 474250 Fax: 01334 474583*
34 acres, grassy, level, mid Mar-Oct, prior booking in peak periods, overnight holding area. Extra charge for electricity, awnings.

456

110 tourers £8.00-10.00 or 110 motors £8.00-10.00. Total Touring Pitches 110. No tents.
12 Holiday Caravans to let, sleep 4-6 £80.00-220.00, total sleeping capacity 72, min. let 3 nights.

Leisure facilities: ♦ ⊕ ►
Take A918 to Anstruther. Site 1½ mls on left.

Key to symbols is on back flap

ST ANDREWS, Fife, Map Ref. 2E3

286

J & C Kirkaldy, Cairnsmill Caravan Park, Largo Road, St Andrews, Fife, KY16 8NN
☎ *(St Andrews) 01334 473604*
20 acres, grassy, level, Apr-Oct, prior booking in peak periods, latest time of arrival 2200, overnight holding area. Extra charge for electricity, awnings.

79 tourers £8.50-9.00 or 79 motors £8.50-9.00 or 10 tents £8.50-9.00.
Total Touring Pitches 80.
5 Holiday Caravans to let, sleep 6 £195.00-210.00, total sleeping capacity 30, min. let 3 nights.

Leisure facilities:
On A915 1 ml S of St Andrews.

INSPECTED

Kinkell Braes Caravan Park
Booking Enquiries: Mrs Y Tilbery, 53 John Street, Cellardyke, Anstruther, Fife, KY10 3BA
☎ *(Anstruther) 01333 310454*
Holiday Caravan to let, sleeps 6 £100.00-210.00, min.let weekend, Apr-Oct.

Leisure facilities:

ST CYRUS, by Montrose, Kincardineshire, Map Ref. 4G12

60

East Bowstrips Caravan Park, St Cyrus, Nr Montrose, Kincardineshire, DD10 0DE
☎ *(St Cyrus) 01674 850328*
4 acres, mixed, Apr-Oct, latest time of arrival 2200, overnight holding area.
Extra charge for electricity, awnings, showers.

30 tourers £5.50-6.50 or 30 motors £5.50-6.50 or 30 tents £4.50-5.50.
Total Touring Pitches 30.
3 Holiday Caravans to let, sleep 4-6 £85.00-200.00, total sleeping capacity 14, min. let 1 night.

Leisure facilities:
From S (Montrose) on A92, enter St Cyrus pass hotel, 1st left, 2nd right.
From N (Aberdeen) on A92, enter St Cyrus and take 1st right, 2nd right.

ST FILLANS, Perthshire, Map Ref. 2A2

270

Loch Earn Caravan Park, Ardtrostan, St Fillans, Perthshire, PH6 2NL
☎ *(St Fillans) 01764 685270*
22 acres, grassy, level, Apr-Oct, prior booking in peak periods,
latest time of arrival 2000. Extra charge for electricity, awnings, showers.

40 tourers £6.50 or 40 motors £6.50. Total Touring Pitches 40. No tents.
Leisure facilities:
From A85 at St.Fillans, take South Loch Earn road. Site is 1.5 mls from A85.

SALEN, Aros, Isle of Mull, Argyll, Map Ref. 1D2

Booking Enquiries: Mrs C MacGillivray, Pennygown Farm, Aros, Isle of Mull, Argyll, PA72
☎ *(Aros) 01680 300335*
Holiday Caravan to let, sleeps 4 £130.00-180.00, min.let 4 nights, Mar-Oct.

🚿 ⌂ ☉ 🚐 ⊟ E wc P 🛒 ⟳ ✕ 🗑 🛢 ♿ 🏇

SANDEND, Banffshire, Map Ref. 4F7

Sandend Caravan Park, Sandend, by Portsoy, Banffshire, AB4
☎ *(Portsoy) 01261 842660*
4 acres, grassy, hard-standing, level, Apr-Oct, latest time of arrival 2300,
overnight holding area. Extra charge for electricity, awnings, showers.

🚿 ⌂ ☉ ▣ ✦ 🚐 E wc P 🛒 ⟳ ✕ 🐕 🐓 🔥 ⛓ 🛢 🦟 ⚲ SP
22 tourers £6.75-7.85 and 4 motors £6.25-7.85 and 6 tents £5.25-6.25.
Total Touring Pitches 32.
3 Holiday Caravans to let, sleep 6-7 £150.00-285.00, total sleeping capacity 19,
min. let weekend.

🚿 ⌂ ☉ ⊟ E wc P 🛒 ⟳ ✕ 🐕 🗑 🛢 ♿ D
Leisure facilities: ▶ 🏌 ⚓ ∪
On main A98 Aberdeen-Inverness road. Between Portsoy/Cullen.

SANDHEAD, Wigtownshire, Map Ref. 1F11

Sands of Luce Caravan Park, Sandhead, by Stranraer, Wigtownshire, DG9 9JN
☎ *(Sandhead) 01776 830456*
Booking Enquiries: Mr & Mrs J W Sime
12 acres, mixed, mid Mar-Oct, prior booking in peak periods, latest time of arrival
2200, overnight holding area. Extra charge for electricity, awnings.

🚿 ⌂ ☉ ▣ ✦ 🚐 🛜 E wc P 🛒 ⟳ ✕ 🐕 🔺 🔥 ⛓ 🛢 🦟 ⚲
26 tourers £5.50-7.00 or 26 motors £5.00-6.50 or 10 tents £5.50-7.00.
Total Touring Pitches 26.
8 Holiday Caravans to let, sleep 4-6 £115.00-240.00, total sleeping capacity 46,
min. let 2 days.

🚿 ⌂ ☉ ⊟ E wc P 🛒 ⟳ ✕ 🐕 🔺 🖳 🗑 🛢 ♿ D
Leisure facilities: ✪ ⚓
From Stranraer take A77/A716 S for 7 mls. Entrance at junction of A716/B7084
approx. 1 ml N of Sandhead.

SCONE, by Perth, Perthshire, Map Ref. 2C2

Scone Palace Camping & Caravanning Park, Scone Racecourse, Scone, Perth, Perthshire, PH2 6BE
☎ *(Scone) 01738 552323 (before 2000)*
Booking Enquiries: Camping & Caravanning Club-TOURERS ONLY,
Greenfields House, Westwood Way, Coventry, CV4 8JH
☎ *(Coventry) 01203 694995 (out of season)* Fax: 01203 694886 *(out of season)*
14 acres, grassy, level, Mar-Oct, prior booking in peak periods, latest time of arrival 2100,
overnight holding area. Extra charge for electricity.

🚿 ⌂ ☉ ▣ ✦ 🚐 E P 🛒 ⟳ ✕ 🐕 🖳 🔺 ⛓ 🛢 🦟 ⚲ ⊞ T
150 tourers £6.73-7.63 or 150 motors £6.73-7.63 or 150 tents £6.73-7.63.
Total Touring Pitches 150.
20 Holiday Caravans to let, sleep 4-8 £110.00-240.00, total sleeping capacity 160,
min. let 2 nights.

🚿 ⌂ ⟶ ☉ ⊟ E wc P 🛒 ⟳ ✕ 🐕 🖳 🔺 🗑 🛢 ♿ ⊞ T D
Leisure facilities: ● ✪ ▶ 🏌 ∪ ✎ ☒ ♦ ⚵ ↯ ⚐ ⚑
From Perth take A93. Turn onto Stormontfield road then
onto drive to racecourse.

Key to symbols
is on back flap

VAT is shown at 17.5%: changes in this rate may affect prices.

SELKIRK, Map Ref. 2E7

Victoria Park Caravan & Camping Site, Victoria Park, Buccleuch Road, Selkirk, TD7 5DN
☎ *(Selkirk) 01750 20897*
3 acres, grassy, hard-standing, level, Apr-Oct, latest time of arrival 2100.
Extra charge for electricity.

🔧 📻 ☉ 🗐 ⚡ 🚐 🛒 E 🚾 P 🛍 ♿ ✕ 🐕 ⚠ 🜂 🎮 🔓 ▣

60 tourers from £5.10 or 60 motors from £5.10 or 60 tents from £5.10.
Total Touring Pitches 60.

Leisure facilities: 🏊 🏰 🎣 🎿 🛩

From S on A7 follow signs from Selkirk market place. From N on A7 turn right s/posted A72(Peebles)/A708(Moffat) at town entrance. From Peebles on A707 follow signs on outskirts, turn L just over river.

SKELMORLIE, Ayrshire, Map Ref. 1G5

Mains Caravan Park, Skelmorlie Mains, Ayrshire, PA17 5EU
☎ *(Wemyss Bay) 01475 520794*
6 acres, mixed, mid Mar-Oct, latest time of arrival 2400, overnight holding area.
Extra charge for electricity, awnings, showers.

🔧 📻 ☉ 🚐 🛒 🖵 E 🚾 P 🛍 ♿ ✕ 🐕 🎠 ⚓ 🜂 🎮 🔓

16 tourers £6.00-7.00 and 10 motors £6.00-7.00 and 70 tents £5.00-6.00.
Total Touring Pitches 96.
10 Holiday Caravans to let, sleep 4-6 £140.00-240.00, total sleeping capacity 60, min. let 2 nights.

🔧 📻 🖵 E 🚾 P 🛍 ♿ ✕ 🐕 🎠 🖵 ⌀ 🗓 🛋 ⚒

Leisure facilities: 🎯 ▸ 🏌 ⛳ U △ ✈ ⚓ 🎿
¹/₂ ml from Skelmorlie off A78 Greenock-Largs road. 4 mls N of Largs.

SOUTHERNESS, Dumfriesshire, Map Ref. 2B10

Lighthouse Leisure

Southerness, Dumfries DG2 8AZ   Tel: (01387) 880277

Escape to tranquillity, by sweeping sandy beaches and magnificent views. 8 acre grass park with new leisure complex, heated pool, sauna etc. overlooking championship golf course with 6 other courses within 15 miles. Mountain bikes for hire. Children's toytown, fishing, amusements, pubs and all facilities.

I D E A L   Q U I E T   F A M I L Y   H O L I D A Y.

Lighthouse Leisure, Southerness, Dumfriesshire, DG2 8AZ
☎ *(Kirkbean) 01387 880277*
8¹/₂ acres, grassy, level, Mar-Oct, prior booking in peak periods.
Extra charge for electricity, awnings.

15 tourers £5.00-6.00 or 15 motors £5.00-6.00 or 15 tents £4.50-6.00.
Total Touring Pitches 15.
5 Holiday Caravans to let, sleep 4-6 £70.00-195.00, total sleeping capacity 30, min. let 1 night.

Leisure facilities:
From Dumfries take A710 S for 15 mls. Turn left at Southerness sign for 2 mls. Park office by first house on right.

Southerness Holiday Village, Southerness, Dumfriesshire, DG2 8BA
☎ *(Kirkbean) 0138788 281/278/256*
60 acres, grassy, Mar-Oct, overnight holding area.
Extra charge for electricity, awnings.

200 tourers £5.75-7.00 or 200 motors £5.75-7.00 or 200 tents £5.75-7.00.
Total Touring Pitches 200.
45 Holiday Caravans to let, sleep 6 £60.00-230.00, total sleeping capacity 270, min. let weekend.

Leisure facilities:
Take A710 out of Dumfries for approx. 15 mls. Southerness signposted to left hand side just through village of Kirkbean.

SPEAN BRIDGE, Inverness-shire, Map Ref. 3H12

INSPECTED

Gairlochy Bay Caravan Site
Booking Enquiries: Mrs M Stevenson, Achnacarry Post Office, Post Office Hse, Spean Bridge, Inverness-shire, PH34 4EJ
☎ *(Spean Bridge) 01397 712718*
4 Holiday Caravans to let, sleep 6-8 £130.00-160.00, total sleeping capacity 30, Apr-Oct.

Leisure facilities:
A82 N Spean Bridge, turn onto B8004 for Gairlochy, 200m right on B8005.

Key to symbols is on back flap

BY SPEAN BRIDGE, Inverness-shire, Map Ref. 3H12

Booking Enquiries: Mrs Catherine Cameron, 2 Balmaglaster, Spean Bridge, Inverness-shire, PH34 4EB
☎ *(Invergarry) 018093 289*
Holiday Caravan to let, sleeps 6 £90.00-160.00, min. let weekend (low season), Jan-Dec.

🔥 📻 🚗 🖵 E 🆆 🅿 🧺 ✕ 🐕 🛄 ∅ 🗑 ♿ 🚲

Leisure facilities: 🔵 ♨ ⚓

Take A82 22 mls N of Fort William. Turn left at Balmaglaster, Kilfinnan road sign. Caravan at fifth house. Approx 1½ mls up this road.

SPEY BAY, Moray, Map Ref. 4E7

Spey Bay Caravan Park, Spey Bay, Fochabers, Moray, IV32 7PJ
☎ *(Fochabers) 01343 820424*
3 acres, grassy, level, Apr-Oct. Extra charge for electricity.

🔥 📻 ☉ 🖥 ✄ 🚗 ⛽ 🖵 E 🆆 🅿 🧺 ✕ 🐕 ⚠ 🍽 Ⓡ 🔔 ♫ 🚙 📞 📅 Ⓓ

17 tourers £6.00 and 5 motors £6.00 and 8 tents £6.00. Total Touring Pitches 30.
Leisure facilities: ● 🌍 ✎ ▶ 🎣
At Fochabers turn off A96 to Spey Bay.

STIRLING, Map Ref. 2A4

Witches Craig Caravan Park, Blairlogie, Stirling, FK9 5PX
☎ *(Stirling) 01786 474947*
5 acres, grassy, hard-standing, level, Apr-Oct, prior booking in peak periods, latest time of arrival 2100. Extra charge for electricity, awnings, showers.

🔥 📻 ☉ 🖥 ✄ 🚗 ⛽ 🖵 E 🆆 🅿 🧺 ⊙ ✕ 🐕 ⚠ 🔔 🚙 📞 Ⓓ

30 tourers £7.50-8.50 and 10 motors £7.50-8.50 and 20 tents £7.50-8.50.
Total Touring Pitches 60.
Leave Stirling take St Andrews road, A91 3 mls E of Stirling.

Booking Enquiries: Mrs E Graham, West Drip Farm, Stirling, FK9 4UJ
☎ *(Stirling) 01786 472523*
2 Holiday Caravans to let, sleep 6-8 £100.00-160.00, total sleeping capacity 14, min. let weekend, Apr-Oct.

🔥 📻 ☉ 🖵 E 🆆 🅿 🧺 ✕ 🐕 🛏 🛄 ∅ 🗑 ♿ † 🚲

Exit M9 at J10 onto A84 and follow signs for Callander.
Cross river, farm road end is third left, about ½ ml.

STRATHPEFFER, Ross-shire, Map Ref. 4A8

Booking Enquiries: Mrs M MacDonald, Glenburn, Heights of Inchvannie, Strathpeffer, Ross-shire, IV14 9AE
☎ *(Strathpeffer) 01997 421381*
2 Holiday Caravans to let, sleep 4-8 £120.00-150.00, total sleeping capacity 14, min. let 2 nights, Apr-Oct.

Ⓜ 🔥 📻 ☉ 🚗 🖵 E 🆆 🅿 🧺 ⊙ ✕ 🐕 🛏 ⚠ 🛄 ∅ 🗑 ♿ 🚲

Take A834 W from Dingwall to Strathpeffer, turn right signposted Acherneed for 1½ mls.

STRATHYRE, Perthshire, Map Ref. 1H3

60

Immervoulin Caravan & Camping Park, Strathyre, Perthshire, FK18 8NJ
☎ *(Strathyre) 01877 384285/384682 Fax: 01877 384295*
5 acres, grassy, sandy, level, Apr-Oct, latest time of arrival 2000.
Extra charge for electricity, awnings, showers.

50 tourers £7.00-8.00 or 50 motors £7.00-8.00 or 50 tents £7.00-8.00.
Total Touring Pitches 50.
Leisure facilities:
On A84 9 mls N of Callander and on southern outskirts of Strathyre

STROMNESS, Orkney, Map Ref. 5A11

30

Point of Ness Caravan & Camping Site, Stromness, Orkney, KW16
Booking Enquiries: Education Department, County Offices, School Place,
Kirkwall, Orkney, KW15 1JG
☎ *(Kirkwall) 01856 873535*
1¹/₂ acres, grassy, sandy, May-Sep, prior booking in peak periods.
Extra charge for electricity, awnings, showers.

30 tourers to £4.50 or 30 motors to £4.50 or 30 tents to £2.10-3.90.
Total Touring Pitches 30.
Turn left on leaving ferry, follow main street to Site.

STRONTIAN, Argyll, Map Ref. 1E1

41

Glenview Caravan Park, Strontian, Argyll, PH36 4JD
☎ *(Strontian) 01967 402123 Fax: 01967 402123*
3 acres, mixed, Apr-Oct, prior booking in peak periods, latest time of arrival 2300.
Extra charge for electricity.

14 tourers £7.50-8.50 or 15 motors £7.50-8.50 or 15 tents £5.50-6.00.
Total Touring Pitches 29.
4 Holiday Caravans to let, sleeps 6 £160.00-230.00, total sleeping capacity 24, min. let weekend.

On A82 Glencoe/Fort William road take Corran Ferry to Ardgour.
Follow A831 to Strontian, turn right at police station, and follow signs.

BY TAIN Ross-shire, Map Ref. 4B7

50

Meikle Ferry Caravan Park, Meikle Ferry, by Tain, Ross-shire, IV19 1JX
☎ *(Tain) 01862 892292*
3¹/₂ acres, grassy, level, Jan-Dec, prior booking in peak periods,
latest time of arrival 2100. Extra charge for electricity, awnings, showers.

20 tourers £6.00-7.00 and 5 motors £6.00-7.00 and 5 tents £5.00-6.00.
Total Touring Pitches 30.
11 Holiday Caravans to let, sleep 4-6 £100.00-220.00, total sleeping capacity 56,
min. let 2 nights.

Leisure facilities:
A9 N from Tain 2 mls, round roundabout Site 150 yds on right.

Key to symbols
is on back flap

VAT is shown at 17.5%: changes in this rate may affect prices.

TARBET, Dunbartonshire, Map Ref. 1G3

Booking Enquiries: Mrs Pat Handy, Blairannaich, Tarbet, Arrochar, Dunbartonshire, G83 7DN
☎ *(Arrochar) 013012 257*
3 Holiday Caravans to let, sleep 6 £125.00-150.00, total sleeping capacity 18, min. let weekend, Mar-Oct.

🔥 ♔ ☉ 🛒 ⊐ E 🆆 🅿 🐾 ↻ ✕ 🐎 ⚠ 🚽 ⊘ 🗓 🛁

Leisure facilities: ▶ ⏌ ⏌ ∪ ☒ ♦ ⚘ ⚭ ⚱

TAYINLOAN, by Tarbert, Argyll, Map Ref. 1D6

POINT SANDS CARAVAN PARK
Tayinloan, Argyll PA29 6XG   Tel: (015834) 263 or 275

Beautiful peaceful seaside park. Superb safe sandy beach opposite Isle of Gigha. Ideal for family holidays, golf, pony-trekking, fishing available in the area. Beach suitable for sailing and windsurfing on site.

Visit the Isles, Gigha, Islay and Arran.

135

Point Sands Caravan Park, Tayinloan, by Tarbert, Argyll, PA29 6XG
☎ *(Tayinloan) 015834 263/275*
14 acres, mixed, Apr-Oct, prior booking in peak periods, latest time of arrival 2000, overnight holding area. Extra charge for electricity, awnings.

🔥 ♔ ☉ 🛒 ⚡ 🛒 🏵 E 🆆 🅿 🐾 ↻ ✕ 🐎 🏛 ⚠ ⛲ ♨ 🔔 ⊞ 🆂🅿

40 tourers £6.50-8.00 or 40 motors £6.00-8.00 or 20 tents £4.00-6.80.
Total Touring Pitches 60.
8 Holiday Caravans to let, sleep 4-8 £115.00-295.00, total sleeping capacity 50, min. let 1 night.

🔥 ♔ ⊐ E 🆆 🅿 🐾 ↻ ✕ 🐎 🏛 ⚠ 🚽 ⊘ 🗓 🛁 ⊞ Ⓓ

Leisure facilities: ✪ ▶ ⏌ ∪
Midway between Campbeltown and Tarbert on A83.

TAYNUILT, Argyll, Map Ref. 1F2

Booking Enquiries: Mrs Jean Campbell, Inverlorn, Taynuilt, Argyll, PA35 1JW
☎ *(Taynuilt) 018662 635*
Holiday Caravan to let, sleeps 4 £90.00-165.00, min. let 3 nights, Easter-Oct.

🔥 ♔ 🛒 ⊐ E 🆆 🅿 🐾 ✕ 🐎 🚽 ⊘ 🗓 🛁 🚲

On A85 road, last house before end of 40 mph sign, Oban side.

THORNHILL, Dumfriesshire, Map Ref. 2B8

Booking Enquiries: Mrs B Maxwell, Druidhall Farm, Thornhill, Dumfriesshire, DG3 4NE
☎ *(Marrburn) 018486 271*
2 Holiday Caravans to let, sleep 6 to £145.00, total sleeping capacity 12, min. let weekend, Mar-Nov.

🔥 ♔ ☉ 🛒 ⊐ E 🆆 🅿 ↻ 🐎 🚽 ⊘ 🗓 🛁 🚲

From Thornhill go to Penpont. Turn right in Penpont at crossroads for Scaur Water. Bear left for 3½ mls. Druidhall sits on T-junction.

THURSO, Caithness, Map Ref. 4C3

Thurso Caravan & Camping Site, Scrabster Road, Thurso, Caithness, KW14 7JY
☎ *(Wick) 01955 3761 Fax: 01955 2481*
Booking Enquiries: Mr J W Robertson, Caithness Dist Council, Council Offices, Wick, Caithness, KW1 4AB
☎ *(Wick) 01955 3761 Fax: 01955 2481*
4¹/₂ acres, mixed, May-Sep, latest time of arrival 2200, overnight holding area.
Extra charge for electricity, awnings.

92 tourers £5.90-6.70 or 92 motors £5.90-6.70 or 50 tents £5.90-6.70.
Total Touring Pitches 92.
Leisure facilities:
On A882 overlooking Thurso Bay and within Burgh boundary, on Smith Terrace.

TOWN YETHOLM, Roxburghshire, Map Ref. 2F7

Kirkfield Caravan Park, Grafton Road, Town Yetholm, Roxburghshire, TD5 8RU
☎ *(Yetholm) 01573420 346 Fax: 01573420 720*
2 acres, grassy, level, Apr-Oct, prior booking in peak periods,
latest time of arrival 2100. Extra charge for electricity, awnings.

15 tourers from £6.00 or 15 motors from £5.50. Total Touring Pitches 15. No tents.
From Kelso take B6352 to Town Yetholm. Turn left at signpost for Kirk Yetholm then
sharp right at old church.

TUMMEL BRIDGE, Perthshire, Map Ref. 2A1

Tummel Valley Holiday Park

Tummel Bridge, Perthshire PH16 5SA
Caravan holiday homes and timber lodges. Tourers. Indoor pool, lounge bar, restaurant, take-away shop, games room, play areas, crazy golf. Nightly entertainment April 28-Oct 1, weekends other dates.
Prices: Lodges from £170-£495 per week.
Caravans from £130-£395 per week.
Short Breaks from £50 for 2 nights. (all inc. VAT)
Contact Parkdean Holidays (0191) 2240500 for brochure.

PITLOCHRY Quote STB

Tummel Valley Holiday Park, Tummel Bridge, Perthshire, PH16 5SA
☎ *(Tummel Bridge) 01882 634221 Fax: 01882 634302*
Booking Enquiries: Parkdean Holidays Ltd, Cragside House, 42a Heaton Road, Newcastle upon Tyne, Tyne & Wear, NE6 1SE
☎ *0191 224 0500 Fax: 0191 224 0490*
55 acres, mixed, Apr-Oct, prior booking in peak periods, latest time of arrival 2300,
overnight holding area. Extra charge for electricity, awnings.

110 tourers £10.50-13.00 or 110 motors £10.50-13.00 or 110 tents £5.00-8.00.
Total Touring Pitches 110.
64 Holiday Caravans to let, sleep 6-8 £130.00-410.00, total sleeping capacity 420,
min. let 2 nights.

Leisure facilities:
Take B8019 to Tummel Bridge, by leaving A9 1¹/₂ mls N of Pitlochry.
The park is 11 mls on left.

Key to symbols
is on back flap

VAT is shown at 17.5%: changes in this rate may affect prices.

ULLAPOOL, Ross-shire, Map Ref. 3G6

45

Ardmair Point Caravan Site & Boat Centre, Ullapool, Ross-shire, IV26 2TN
☎ (Ullapool) 01854 612054 Fax: 01854 612757
3¹/₂ acres, grassy, level, May-Sep, latest time of arrival 2200.
Extra charge for electricity, awnings, showers.

🔧 📷 ⊙ 🗑 ∥ ⟨🖩 E 🚾 P ⟳ ✕ 🐕 Ⓡ ⛴ ♨ ♨ 🔆 👤 Ⓓ

45 tourers £5.60-7.50 or 45 motors £5.60-7.50 or 45 tents £5.60-7.50.
Total Touring Pitches 45.

Leisure facilities: 🛶 ⛰ 🎣 ⛵
3¹/₂ mls N of Ullapool on A835. Enter next to telephone kiosk.

INSPECTED

Booking Enquiries: Mr Roderick Stewart, 58 Rhue, Ullapool, Ross-shire, IV26 2TJ
☎ (Ullapool) 01854 612435
Holiday Caravan to let, sleeps 4 £80.00-100.00, Apr-Oct.

Ⓜ 🔧 📷 ⊙ ⟱ E 🚾 P ✕ 🐕 ⊘ 🗑 ♨ 🛷

WHITHORN, Wigtownshire, Map Ref. 1H11

27

H

Castlewigg Caravan Park, Whithorn, Wigtownshire, DG8 8DP
☎ (Whithorn) 01988 500616
4 acres, grassy, sheltered, Jan-Dec, prior booking in peak periods, latest time of arrival 2300, overnight holding area. Extra charge for electricity, awnings, showers.

🔧 📷 ⊙ 🗑 ⟨🖩 E 🚾 P 🛒 ⟳ ✕ 🐕 ⨆ ⚠ 🍽 Ⓡ ⛴ ♨ 🔆 👤 SP

15 tourers £6.00-7.00 or 15 motors £6.00-7.00 or 15 tents £5.00-6.00.
Total Touring Pitches 15.
7 Holiday Caravans to let, sleep 6 £100.00-190.00, total sleeping capacity 42, min. let 1 day.

🔧 📷 ⊙ 🅿 ⟱ E 🚾 🛒 ⟳ ✕ 🐕 ⨆ ⚠ 🖥 ⊘ 🗑 ♨

Leisure facilities: ⊕ ▶ 🏸 🛶 ∪ ⛰
From roundabout at Newton Stewart take A714 turning right just before Wigtown, continue through villages of Kirkinner and Sorbie, site situated approx.
1¹/₂ mls from Whithorn.

TELEPHONE DIALLING CODES

On 16 April 1995 all UK area codes starting **0** will start **01**.

From August 1994 until 16 April 1995, the new codes will be run in parallel with the old ones.
If you experience difficulty in connecting a call, please call Directory Enquiries – **192** – for advice. Please note: A charge will be made for this service when using a private phone.

Important: Prices stated are estimates and may be subject to amendments

WHITING BAY, Isle of Arran, Map Ref. 1F7

COOPER ANGUS PARK

Escape to an unspoilt yet easily accessible Island warmed by the gulf stream. Luxury caravans for hire on holiday park set in magnificent scenery by waters edge. Heated swimming pool. *Colour brochure on request.*

Whiting Bay, Isle of Arran KA27 8QP
Telephone: (01770) 700381   Fax: (01770) 700370

45

Cooper Angus Park, Whiting Bay, Isle of Arran, KA17 8QP
☎ *(Whiting Bay) 01770 700381 Fax: 01770 700370*
4¹/₂ acres, grassy, level, sheltered, Mar-Oct, prior booking in peak periods.

20 Holiday Caravans to let, sleep 4-6 from £140.00, total sleeping capacity 110, min.let weekend, Mar-Oct.

Leisure facilities: ⋏ ● ►
On disembarkation from ferry head S. 8¹/₂ mls to Whiting Bay. Park is on sea shore.

Scotland for Golf . . .

Find out more about golf in Scotland. There's more to it than just the championship courses so get in touch with us now for information on the hidden gems of Scotland.

Write to: **Information Unit, Scottish Tourist Board, 23 Ravelston Terrace, Edinburgh EH4 3EU or call: 0131-332 2433**

QUALITY
YOU WANT IT. WE OFFER IT.

Key to symbols
is on back flap

VAT is shown at 17.5%: changes in this rate may affect prices.

The Thistle Award for quality is awarded annually by the Scottish Tourist Board only after rigorous inspection. This inspection is your gauarantee of the highest standard in your Caravan Holiday-Home.
Thistle Award Caravans are located on top quality parks throughout Scotland offering you a choice of locations in whichto enjoy your caravan holiday.
Each Thistl Award Caravan offers you a relaxing, well appointed living area, from one to three separate bedrooms, a fully fitted kitchen with full size cooker and fridge, and of course, bathroom or shower with w.c. Thistle Award Caravans are an elite group and as such are rapidly booked. So don't delay.
Look for the sign that sets the standard and book your carefree holiday.

Appin Holiday Homes
Appin
Argyll
PA39 4BQ
Tel: 0163173 287

Argyll Caravan Park
Invreraray
Argyll
PA32 8XT
Tel: 01499 2285

Barlochan Caravan Park
Palnackie, by Castle Douglas
Kirkcudbrightshire
DG7 1PF
Tel: 01556 600256

Black Rock Caravan Park
Evanton
Ross-shire
IV6 9UN
Tel: 01349 830917

Blair Castle Caravan Park
Blair Atholl
Perthshire
PH18 5SR
Tel: 01796 481263

Blairgowrie Caravan Park
Blairgowrie
Perthshire
PH10 7AL
Tel: 01250 872941

Braidhaugh Caravan Park
Crieff
Perthshire
PH7 4HP
Tel: 01764 652951

Brighouse Bay Holiday Park
Kirkcudbright
Kirkcudbrightshire
DG6 4TS
Tel: 015577 267

Bunchrew Caravan &
   Camping Park
Inverness
Inverness-shire
IV3 6TD
Tel: 01463 237802

Campgrounds of Scotland
Boat of Garten
Inverness-shire
PH24 3BN
Tel: 01479 831652

Campgrounds of Scotland,
   Coylumbridge
Aviemore
Inverness-shire
PH22 1QU
Tel: 01479 810120

Cannich Caravan and Camping
   Park
Cannich, by Beauly
Inverness-shire
IV4 7LN
Tel: 01456 415364

Cock Inn Caravan Park
Auchenmalg, Newton Stewart
Wigtownshire
DG8 0JT
Tel: 015815 227

Craigtoun Meadows
   Holiday Park
St Andrews
Fife
KY16 8PQ
Tel: 01334 75959

Creetown Caravan Park
Creetown, Nr Newton Stewart
Wigtownshire
CG8 7HU
Tel: 01671 820377

Crieff Holiday Village
Crieff
Perthshire
PH7 4JN
Tel: 01764 653513

Cruivend Holiday Park
Beauly
Inverness-shire
IV4 7BE
Tel: 01463 782367

Delnies Woods Caravan Park
Nairn
Nairnshire
IV12 5NT
Tel: 01667 455281

Drumlochart Caravan Park
Lochnaw, by Stranraer
Wigtownshire
DG9 0RN
Tel: 01776 870232

Erigmore House Holiday Park
Dunkeld
Perthshire
PH8 9XX
Tel: 01350 727236

Feughside Caravan Park
Banchory
Kincardineshire
AB31 3NT
Tel: 01330 850669

Galloway Point Holiday Park
Portpatrick
Wigtownshire
DG9 9AA
Tel: 01776 810561

Glen Dochart Caravan Park
Luib, by Crianlarich
Perthshire
FK20 8QT
Tel: 01567 820637

Glendaruel Caravan Park
Glendaruel
Argyll
PA22 3AB
Tel: 0136982 267

Glenluce Caravan Park
Glenluce
Wigtownshire
DG8 0QR
Tel: 015813 00412

Glenview Caravan Park
Strontian
Argyll
PH36 4JD
Tel: 01967 402123

Grannies Heilan Hame Holiday
  Park
Embo, Dornoch
Sutherland
IV25 3QD
Tel: 01862 810383

Hillhead Caravan Park
Kintore
Aberdeenshire
AB51 0YX
Tel: 01467 632809

Inverbeg Holiday Park
Inverbeg, by Luss
Dunbartonshire
G83 8PD
Tel: 01436 860267

Invercoe Caravans
Glencoe
Argyll
PA39 4HP
Tel: 018552 210

Jedwater Caravan Park
Jedburgh
Roxburghshire
TD8 6QS
Tel: 01835 840219

Kippford Caravan Park
Kippford
Kirkcudbrightshire
DG5 4LF
Tel: 01556 620636

Linnhe Caravan Park
Fort William
Inverness-shire
PH33 7NL
Tel: 01397 772376

Littlewood Holiday Park
Montrose
Angus
DD10 9LE
Tel: 01674 672973

Loch Ken Holiday Park
Parton, Castle Douglas
Kircudbrightshire
DG7 3NE
Tel: 016447 0282

Loch Lomond Holiday Park
Inveruglas, by Tarbet
Dunbartonshire
G83 7DN
Tel: 013014 224

Lochgilphead Caravan Park
Lochgilphead
Argyll
PA31 8MX
Tel: 01546 602003

Lochy Caravan Park
Fort William
Inverness-shire
PH33 7NF
Tel: 01397 703446

Middlemuir Park
Tarbolton, Ayr
Ayrshire
KA5 5NR
Tel: 01292 541647

Mortonhall Caravan Park
Edinburgh
EH16 6TJ
Tel: 0131 664 1533

Muasdale Holiday Park
Muasdale
Argyll
PA29 6XD
Tel: 01583 2207

Nairn Lochloy Holiday Park
Nairn
Nairnshire
IV12 4PH
Tel: 01667 453764

Northburn Holiday Home Park
Eyemouth
Berwickshire
TD14 5BE
Tel: 018907 51050

Old Mill Caravan Park
Forres
Morayshire
IV36 0TD
Tel: 01309 641244

Park of Brandedleys
Crocketford
Dumfriesshire
DG2 8RG
Tel: 01556 690250

Peniver Sands Holiday Park
Peniver, by Campbeltown
Argyll
PA28 6QP
Tel: 01586 552262

Pitgrudy Caravan Park
Dornoch
Sutherland
IV25 3HY
Tel: 01862 82253

Point Sands
Tayinloan, by Tarbert
Argyll
PA29 6XG
Tel: 015834 263

Resipole Farm Caravan Park
Resipole, by Acharacle
Argyll
PH36 4HX
Tel: 01967 431235

Rosneath Castle Caravan Park
by Helensburgh
Dunbartonshire
G84 0QS
Tel: 01436 831208/831391

Sands Holiday Centre
Gairloch
Ross-shire
IV21 2DL
Tel: 01445 712152

Scone Palace Caravan Park
Perth
Perthshire
PH2 6BD
Tel: 01738 523108

Scoutscroft Holiday Centre
Coldingham
Berwickshire
TD14 5NB
Tel: 018907 71338

Seaward Caravan Park
Kirkcudbright
Kirkcudbrightshire
DG6 4TS
Tel: 01557 331079

Seton Sands Holiday Village
Longniddry
East Lothian
EH32 0QF
Tel: 01875 813333

Silver Ladies Caravan Park
Strachan, by Banchory
Kincardineshire
AB31 3NL
Tel: 01330 822800

Silver Sands Leisure Park
Lossiemouth
Morayshire
IV31 6SP
Tel: 01343 813262

Stratheck Caravan Park
Loch Eck, by Dunoon
Argyll
PA23 8SG
Tel: 0136984 472

Sundrum Castle Holiday Park
Coylton, by Ayr
Ayrshire KA6 6HX
Tel: 01292 570057
Tayock Caravan Park
Montrose
Angus
DD10 9LE
Tel: 01674 673253

The Monks' Muir
Haddington
East Lothian
EH41 3SB
Tel: 01620 860340

Thurston Manor Holiday Park
Innerwick, by Dunbar
East Lothian
EH42 1SA
Tel: 01368 840643

Torvean Caravan Park
Inverness
Highland
IV3 6JL
Tel: 01463 220582

Trossachs Holiday Park
Aberfoyle
Perthshire
FK8 3SA
Tel: 01877 382614

Tullichewan Caravan Park
Balloch, Loch Lomond
Dunbartonshire
G83 8QP
Tel: 01389 759475

Tummel Valley Holiday Park
Tummel Bridge
Perthshire
PH16 5SA
Tel: 01882 634221

Wemyss Bay Holiday Park
Wemyss Bay
Renfrewshire
PA18 6BA
Tel: 01475 520812

The following parks provide purpose-built toilet and washing facilities for the disabled. However, it is recommended that customers contact parks to ensure that facilities meet their own particular requirements.

Aberfeldy Caravan Park
Aberfeldy
Perthshire
Tel: 01887 820662

Aberlour Gardens Caravan Park
Aberlour-on-Spey
Moray
Tel: 01340 871586

Aden Caravan Park
Mintlaw
Aberdeenshire
Tel: 01771 623460

Aird Donald Caravan Park
Stranraer
Wigtownshire
Tel: 01776 702025

Ardgartan Campsite
Arrochar
Dunbartonshire
Tel: 013012 293

Ardmair Point Caravan Park
Ullapool
Ross-shire
Tel: 01854 612054

Argyll Caravan Park
Inveraray
Argyll
Tel: 01499 2285

Arran View Caravan Park
Heads of Ayr, Ayr
Ayrshire
Tel: 01292 265141

Auchenlarie Holiday Farm
Gatehouse-of-Fleet
Kirkcudbrightshire
Tel: 01557 840251

Auchterarder Caravan Park
Auchterarder
Perthshire
Tel: 01764 63119

Ballater Caravan Park
Ballater
Kincardineshire
Tel: 013397 55727

Banff Links Caravan Park
Banff
Grampian
tel: 01261 812228

Barlochan Caravan Park
Palnackie, by Castle Douglas
Kirkcudbrightshire
Tel: 01556 600256

Black Rock Caravan Park
Evanton
Ross-shire
Tel: 01349 830917

Blair Castle Caravan Park
Blair Atholl
Perthshire
Tel: 01796 481263

Braidhaugh Caravan Park
Crieff
Perthshire
Tel: 01764 652951

Brighouse Bay Holiday Park
Kirkcudbright
Kirkcudbrightshire
Tel: 015577 267

Bught Caravan Park
Inverness
Tel: 01463 236920

Cairnryan Caravan Park
Cairnryan
Wigtownshire
Tel: 01581 200231

Cairnsmill Caravan Park
St Andrews
Fife
Tel: 01334 73604

Callander Holiday Park
Callander
Perthshire
Tel: 01877 330265

Campgrounds of Scotland
Boat of Garten
Inverness-shire
Tel: 01479 831652

Camping & Caravanning Club Site
Scone
Perthshire
Tel: 01738 52323

Camping & Caravanning Club Site
Balmaha, by Drymen
Stirlingshire
Tel: 0136087 236

Camping & Caravanning Club Site
Dingwall
Ross-shire
Tel: 01349 62236

Camping & Caravanning Club Site
Moffat
Dumfriesshire
Tel: 01683 20436

Camping & Caravanning Club Site
Culzean Castle
Ayrshire
Tel: 016556 627

Camping & Caravanning Club Site
Campbeltown
Argyll
Tel: 0158681 366

Cashel Campsite
Rowardennan, by Balmaha
Stirlingshire
Tel: 01360 87234

Castle Cary Holiday Park
Creetown
Wigtownshire
Tel: 01671 820264

Castle Point Caravan Site
Rockcliffe, by Dalbeattie
Kirkcudbrightshire
Tel: 01556 630248

Clayton Caravan Park
St Andrews
Fife
Tel: 01334 870242

Cleeve Caravan Park
Perth
Perthshire
Tel: 01738 39521

Cobleland Campsite
Gartmore, by Aberfoyle
Perthshire
Tel: 01877 382392

Cock Inn Caravan Park
Auchenmalg, Newton Stewart
Wigtownshire
Tel: 015815 227

Coldingham Caravan Park
Coldingham
Berwickshire
Tel: 018907 71316

Cot House Caravan Park
Kilmun, by Dunoon
Argyll
Tel: 0136984 351

Coulmore Bay Caravan Park
Kessock
Ross-shire
Tel: 0146373 322/212

Craigendmuir Park
Stepps, Glasgow
Tel: 0141 779 4159

Craigie Gardens Caravan Club Site
Ayr
Ayrshire
Tel: 01292 264909

Craigtoun Meadows Holiday Park
St Andrews
Fife
Tel: 01334 75959

Creetown Caravan Park
Creetown, nr Newton Stewart
Wigtownshire
Tel: 01671 820377

Cressfield Caravan Park
Ecclefechan
Dumfriesshire
Tel: 01576 300702

Croft Inn Caravan Park
Melvich
Sutherland
Tel: 016413 262

Croftnacarn Caravan Park
Boat of Garten
Inverness-shire
Tel: 01309 672051

Crossburn Caravan Park
Peebles
Tel: 01721 720501

Crunachy Caravan & Camping Park
Taynuilt, nr Oban
Argyll
Tel: 018662 612

Culloden Moor Caravan Club Site
Culloden Moor
Inverness-shire
Tel: 01463 790625

Dornoch Links Caravan & Camping
Site
Dornoch
Sutherland
Tel: 01862 810423

Dovecot Caravan Park
by Laurencekirk
AB30 1QL
Tel: 01674 840630

Drumshademuir Caravan Park
by Glamis
Angus
Tel: 01575 573284

Dunnikier Caravan Park
Kirkcaldy
Fife
Tel: 01592 267563

Esplanade Caravan Park
Fraserburgh
Aberdeenshire
Tel: 01346 510041

Faskally Caravan Park
Faskally, Pitlochry
Perthshire
Tel: 01796 472007

Feughside Caravan Park
Banchory
Kincardineshire
Tel: 01330 850669

Gairloch Caravan & Camping Park
Gairloch
Ross-shire
Tel: 01445 2373

Gart Caravan Park
Callander
Perthshire
Tel: 01877 330002

Glen Nevis Holiday Caravans
Fort William
Inverness-shire
Tel: 01397 702191

Glendaruel Caravan Park
Glendaruel
Argyll
Tel: 0136982 267

Glenmore Camping & Caravan Park
Glenmore, Aviemore
Inverness-shire
Tel: 01479 861271

Haughton Caravan Park
Alford
Aberdeenshire
Tel: 019755 62107

Hillhead Caravan Park
Kintore
Aberdeenshire
Tel: 01467 632809

Hoddom Castle Caravan Park
Lockerbie
Dumfriesshire
Tel: 01576 300251

Immervoulin Caravan &
Camping Park
Strathyre
Perthshire
Tel: 01877 384285/384682

Invercoe Caravans
Glencoe
Argyll
Tel: 018552 210

Invernahavon Holiday Park
Newtonmore
Inverness-shire
Tel: 01540 673534

John O'Groats Caravan Park
John O'Groats
Caithness
Tel: 01955 81329

Kenmore Caravan & Camping Park
Kenmore, Aberfeldy
Perthshire
Tel: 01887 830226

Kessock Road Caravan Park
Fraserburgh
Grampian
Tel: 01346 510041

Kilvrecht Campsite
Kinloch Rannoch
Perthshire
Tel: 01350 727204

Lagganbeg Caravan Park
Gartocharn, by Balloch
Dunbartonshire
Tel: 01389 830281

Laxdale Holiday Park
Laxdale, Stornoway
Lewis, Western Isles
Tel: 01851 703234

Letham Feus Caravan Park
Letham Feus, by Leven
Fife
Tel: 01333 350323

Little France Caravan Park
Edinburgh
Tel: 0131 666 2326

Loch Ken Holiday Park
Parton, Castle Douglas
Kirkcudbrightshire
Tel: 016447 0282

Loch Lomond Holiday Park
Inveruglas, by Tarbet
Dunbartonshire
Tel: 013014 224

Lochside Caravan Park
Forfar
Angus
Tel: 01307 464201

Merrick Caravan Park
Newton Stewart
Wigtownshire
Tel: 01671 840280

Milton of Fonab Caravan Park
Pitlochry
Perthshire
Tel: 01796 472882

Mortonhall Caravan Park
Edinburgh
Tel: 0131 664 1533

Mosshall Farm Caravan Park
Blackburn
West Lothian
Tel: 01501 762318

Nether Craig Caravan Park
By Alyth, Blairgowrie
Perthshire
Tel: 01575 560204

New England Bay Caravan Club Site
Stranraer
Wigtownshire
Tel: 01776 860275

Newhouse Caravan & Camping Park
Lanark
Strathclyde
Tel: 01555 870228

North Ledaig Caravan Park
Connel, by Oban
Argyll
Tel: 01631 71291

Northburn Holiday Home Park
Eyemouth
Berwickshire
Tel: 018907 51050

Oban Divers Caravan Park
Oban
Argyll
Tel: 01631 62755

Park of Brandedleys
Crocketford
Dumfriesshire
Tel: 01556 690250

Peterhead Caravan Park
Peterhead
Grampian
Tel: 01779 473358

Pickaquoy Caravan & Camping Site
Kirkwall
Orkney
Tel: 01856 872311

Point Sands
Tayinloan, by Tarbert
Argyll
Tel: 015834 263

Point of Ness Caravan &
  Camping Site
Stromness
Orkney
Tel: 01856 873

Resipole Farm Caravan Park
Resipole, by Acharacle
Argyll
Tel: 01967 431235

River Tilt Leisure Park
Blair Atholl
Perthshire
Tel: 01796 481467

Riverside Caravan Park
Elgin
Moray
Tel: 01343 542813

Rosehearty Caravan Park
Rosehearty, by Fraserburgh
Grampian
Tel: 013467 571658

Rosneath Castle Caravan Park
by Helensburgh
Dunbartonshire
Tel: 01436 831208/831391

Sandend Caravan Park
Sandend, by Portsoy
Banffshire
Tel: 01261 842660

Sands of Luce Caravan Park
Stranraer
Wigtownshire
Tel: 01776 830456

Sauchope Links Caravan Park
Crail
Fife
Tel: 01333 450460

Scone Palace Caravan Park
Perth
Perthshire
Tel: 01738 523108

Seaward Caravan Park
Kirkcudbright
Kirkcudbrightshire
Tel: 01557 331079

Seton Sands Holiday Village
Longniddry
East Lothian
Tel: 01875 813333

Shieling Holidays
Craignure
Isle of Mull, Argyll
Tel: 016802 496/016802 812496

Slatebarns Caravan Park
Roslin
Midlothian
Tel: 0131 440 2192

South Links Caravan Park
Montrose
Angus
Tel: 01674 672026

Spey Bay Caravan Park
Spey Bay, by Fochabers
Moray
Tel: 01343 820424

Strathclyde Country Park
Motherwell
Lanarkshire
Tel: 01698 266155

Tayview Holiday Park
Dundee
Tayside
Tel: 01382 532837

Thurso Caravan & Camping Park
Thurso
Caithness
Tel: 01955 3761, ext 241

Thurston Manor Holiday Park
Innerwick, by Dunbar
East Lothian
Tel: 01368 840643

Torvean Caravan Park
Inverness
Highland
Tel: 01463 220582

Tullichewan Caravan Park
Balloch, Loch Lomond
Dunbartonshire
Tel: 01389 759475

Turriff Caravan Park
Turriff
Grampian
Tel: 01888 62205/62779

Victoria Park
Selkirk
Selkirkshire
Tel: 01750 20897

Wairds Park Caravan Park
Johnshaven
Kincardineshire
Tel: 01561 362395

Witches Craig Caravan Park
Stirling
Tel: 01786 474947

Woodlands Caravan Park
Carnoustie
Angus
Tel: 01241 853246

Yellowcraig Caravan Club Site
Dirleton
East Lothian
Tel: 01620 850217

The following parks provide accommodation for the disabled in specially designed or adapted caravan holiday-homes

Argyll Caravan Park
Inveraray
Argyll
Tel: 01499 2285

Arran View Caravan Park
Heads of Ayr, Ayr
Ayrshire
Tel: 01292 265141

Blair Castle Caravan Park
Blair Atholl
Perthshire
Tel: 01796 481263

Brighouse Bay Holiday Park
Kirkcudbright
Kirkcudbrightshire
Tel: 01557 267

Bught Caravan Park
Inverness
Tel: 01463 236920

Cairnryan Caravan Park
Cairnryan
Wigtownshire
Tel: 01581 200231

Dalraddy Holiday Park
Aviemore
Inverness-shire
Tel: 01479 810330

East Bowstrips Caravan Park
St Cyrus, nr Montrose
Kincardineshire
Tel: 01674 850328

Loch Ken Holiday Park
Parton, Castle Douglas
Kirkcudbrightshire
Tel: 016447 0282

Nairn Lochloy Holiday Park
Nairn
Nairnshire
Tel: 01667 453764

Point Sands
Tayinloan, by Tarbert
Argyll
Tel: 015834 263

Seton Sands Holiday Village
Longniddry
East Lothian
Tel: 0875 813333

Shieling Holidays
Craignure
Isle of Mull, Argyll
016802 496/016802 812496

Tantallon Rhodes Caravan Park
North Berwick
East Lothian
Tel: 01620 893348

CUPAR, Fife
St Andrews Motorhomes Ltd
Cairngreen
Pitscottie Road
Cupar
Fife
KY15 5SY
Tel: (01334) 655572
Fax: (01334) 655572
6 Towing caravans, 4 and 5 berth, 14ft-15ft
Price range: from £37 per day, from £137-£240 per week
8 Motor homes, 2-6 berth
Price range: from £34 per night, from £100-£605 per week
Also camping gear available for hire.

FALKIRK, Stirlingshire
Jandi Caravan and Trailer Hire
"Craigavon"
Avonbridge
Falkirk
FK1 2JZ
Tel: (01324) 861303
6 Towing caravans, 4 and 5 berth, 12ft-17ft
Prices: on application for weekend hire, from £120 per week according to season/specification.
Also camping gear available for hire.

GOREBRIDGE, Midlothian
Lothian Caravanette Hire
Newtonloan
Gorebridge
Midlothian
EH23 4LZ
Tel: (01875) 820031
Fax: (01875) 340006
12 Motor homes, 4, 5 and 6 berth
Price range: from £55-£75 per day, from £110-£150 per weekend, from £245-£535 per week

GOUROCK, Renfrewshire
Cabervans, Caberfeidh
Cloch Road, Gourock
Inverclyde
PA19 1BA
Tel: (01475) 638775
Fax: (01475) 638775
4 Towing caravans, 5 berth, 16ft
Price range: from £35 per day, from £70 per weekend, from £225 per week
14 Motor homes, 2-7 berth
Price range: from £70 per day, from £140 per weekend, from £235-£770 per week

KIRKCALDY, Fife
Wallace Caravans (Kirkcaldy)
Thornton Road
Kirkcaldy
Fife KY1 3NW
Tel: (01592) 774265
Fax: (01592) 630607
5 Towing caravans, 2, 4 and 5 berth, 12ft, 14ft and 16ft
Prices: on application for weekly hire.

LARKHALL, Lanarkshire
Brown's Motorcaravan Hire
Garrion Bridge, near Larkhall
Strathclyde ML9 2UD
Tel: (01698) 886255/372543
Fax: (01698) 886255
7 Motor homes, 4-6 berths
Price range: £295-£595 per week, includes insurance and unlimited mileage.
Also camping gear available for hire.

MOTHERWELL, Lanarkshire
Strathclyde Caravans Ltd
341 Windmillhill Street
Motherwell
ML1 2UB
Tel: (01698) 269418
Fax: (01698) 276144
6 Towing caravans, 4 berth, 14 ft
Prices: £120.75 per weekend, £210 per week.

CAMPING AND CARAVAN PARKS

Aberlour Gardens Caravan Park, by Aberlour
Aden Country Park Caravan Park, Mintlaw
Aird Donald Caravan Park, Stranraer
Anderson Road Caravan Park, Ballater
Ardgartan Loch Long Campsite, Ardgarrtan
  by Arrochar
Balcomie Links Caravan Park, Crail
Banff Links Caravan Park, Banff
Barnsoul Farm Park, by Crocketford
Broomfield Holiday Park, Ullapool
Burgh HaughCaravan Site, Inverbervie
Burghead Beach Caravan Park, Burghead
Cairnryan Caravan & Chalet Park, Cairnryan
Chesterfield Caravan Site, Cockburnspath
Cot House Caravan Site, Dunoon
Coulmore Bay Caravan Park, North Kessock
Cowal Caravan Park, Dunoon
Craigie Gardens Caravan Club Site, Ayr
Croyburnfoot Holiday Park, Maybole
Culloden Moor Caravan Club Site,
  Culloden Moor
Drumlochart Caravan Park, Stranraer
East Balthangie Farm Caravan Park,
  Cuminestown
East Beach Caravan Park, Lossiemouth
Esplanade Caravan Park,Fraserburgh
Findochty Caravan Park, Findochty
The Invercauld Caravan Club Site, Braemar
Keith Caravan Park, Keith
Kessock Road Caravan Park, Fraserburgh
Letham Feus Caravan Site, Letham Feus,
  by Leven
Logie Park Caravan Park, Cullen
Lovat Bridge Caravan Site, Beauly
New England Bay Caravan Club Site,
  Drummore, by Stranraer
Messers P G & K A Newton, Etterick Valley
Peterhead Caravan Park, Peterhead
Portnadoran Caravan Site, Arisaig
Portsoy Caravan Park, Portsoy
Queen Elizabeth Caravan Park, Stonehaven
Riverside Chalets Caravan Park, Contin
Rosehearty Caravan Park, Rosehearty,
  by Fraserburgh
Sauchope Links Caravan Park, Crail
Skeldon Caravans, Hoolybush, by Ayr
Springwood Caravan Park, Kelso
St Monans Caravan Park, St Monans

Strathclyde Park Caravan & Camping Site,
  Motherwell
Tayport Caravan Park, Tayport
Thirlestane Castle Caravan & Camping Site,
  Lauder
Turriff Caravan Park, Turriff
West Lodge Caravan Park, Comrie
Yellowcraig Caravan Club Site, Dirleton,
  North Berwick

HOLIDAY CARAVANS

Mrs Sykes, north Wald
Mrs W Jacob, Longniddry
Wemyss Bay Caravan Park, Wemyss Bay
Mr & Mrs Begg, by Banchory
Butt Lodge, Lochranza
Mrs M Copland, Harray
Mrs Dinnie, Aboyne
Mrs Marie Flaws, Evie
Mrs K Foster, Abriachan
Mr & Mrs Gray, Tomatin
Mr D Green, Daviot (East)
Mrs Nancy Hendry, by Elgin
Mrs K Morgan, Sandwick
Mrs M B Kettles, Longforgan, by Dundee
Pamela Hopkins, Lochearnhead
Mrs Leisk, Birsay
Mrs M Newlands, Lochinver
W A MacLeod, Inverness
Mrs McNair, Ford, by Lochgilphead
Mrs L MacRae, Inverness
Mrs Anne MacSween, Portree
Mr John Mackenzie, Staffin
Mrs E Martin, Lairg
Mrs E McCluskey, North Kessock
Mr D McNicol, Bridge of Allan
Mrs J E Oliphant, by Elgin
Mrs M C Payne, Kiltarlity
Mrs B Pirie, Orphir
Mrs M M Ritchie, Beauly
Mrs A Robertson, Oban
Mrs Salisbury, by Inverurie
Mrs Swannie, Stenness
Elsie Walker, Port William
Mrs M Wards, Rendall
Mrs R White, Longniddry
Mrs Wishart, Luss

Scottish parks win Calor 'green' Awards

When the Calor Caravan Park Awards were introduced in 1986 they created quite a stir, being the first awards aimed at encouraging the environmental aspects of park design and management.

The Calor scheme is run in conjunction with the Scottish Tourist Board, the British Holiday & Home Parks Association (BH & HPA), and the National Caravan Council (NCO). As only the highest graded parks are eligible it means that the caravanner or camper staying at a Calor 'green' Award park can expect not only top grade park, but also particular attention to have been paid to a number of environmental matters:

★ Screening of caravans.

★ Use of trees and shrubs to screen central facilities, toilets, etc.

★ Imagination in the use of trees, shrubs, flowers, water, rocks and other natural elements.

In short, making the park an extra special place at which to stay.

The 'green' Awards take the form of cash prizes for environmental projects to improve parks even more, and certificates for the 'Best Park in Scotland' and the 'Most Improved Park in Scotland' which are awarded each year.

Look for these winners in Scotland – they each have something really special to offer:

Best Park in Scotland.

1995: Park of Brandedleys, Crocketford, Dumfriesshire DG2 8RG

1994: Craigtoun Meadows Holiday Park, Mount Melville, St Andrews, Fife KY16 8PQ

Most Improved Park in Scotland.

1995: Campgrounds of Scotland, Coylumbridge, Aviemore Inverness-shire PH22 1QU

1994: Delnies Woods Caravan Park, Nairn IV12 5NT

AYR

Sundrum Castle Holiday Park

COYLTON, AYRSHIRE   Tel: (01292) 570057

Indoor pool, games room, snooker, pool, darts, arcade, play parks, tennis, kiddies' club, discos. "Talk of Ayr" nightclub. Bars, dining and take-away service. One, two and three bedroom. **Prices: £80-£385 per week.** Short breaks from £50 for two nights (incl. VAT).

Contact Parkdean Holidays (0191) 2240500 for brochure.

✓ ✓ ✓ ✓

Nr INVERNESS

Cannich Caravan & Camping Park

Cannich by Beauly, Inverness IV4 7LN
Tel: (01456) 415364   Fax: (01456) 415263

Situated in the heart of the Highlands. Close to Glen Affric and Loch Ness. Superb fishing in the area. Mountain bikes on site for hire. Site facilities include toilets, showers, laundry, T.V.room, electric hook-up and childrens' play area. Pets welcome. Statics for hire daily or weekly.

BOOKS TO HELP YOU

SCOTLAND: HOTELS AND GUEST HOUSES 1995 £8.50

Over 1,600 places to stay in Scotland, from luxury hotels to budget-priced guest houses. Details of prices and facilities, with location maps. Completely revised each year. Includes Grading and Classification quality assurance throughout.

SCOTLAND: BED AND BREAKFAST 1995 £5.90

Over 1,500 B&B establishments throughout Scotland offering inexpensive accommodation. The perfect way to enjoy a budget trip – and meet Scottish folk in their own homes. Details of prices and facilities, with location maps. Completely revised each year. Includes Grading and Classification quality assurance.

SCOTLAND: SELF CATERING ACCOMMODATION 1995 £6.20

Over 1,200 cottages, apartments, houses and chalets to let – many in scenic areas. Details of prices and facilities, with location maps. Completely revised each year. Includes Grading and Classification quality assurance. Full colour throughout.

SCOTLAND: CAMPING AND CARAVAN PARKS 1995 £4.40

Over 250 parks detailed with prices, available facilities and other useful information. Parks inspected under the British Holiday Parks Grading Scheme. Also includes caravan holiday homes for hire. Location maps. Completely revised each year. Entries graded.

ENJOY SCOTLAND PACK £8.40

A handy plastic wallet containing the Scottish Tourist Board's Touring Map of Scotland (5 miles to inch) showing historic sites, gardens, museums, beaches and other places of interest. Enclosed with its Touring Guide to Scotland, which gives locations and details of these places, as well as opening times and admission charges. Details of access for disabled visitors.

TOURING MAP OF SCOTLAND £3.60

As above, available separately.

TOURING GUIDE TO SCOTLAND £4.80

As above, available separately.

POSTERS

A series of colourful posters is available, illustrating a wide range of Scotland's attractions.

All posters printed on high quality paper and the entire range is also available with a plastic coating for extra hard wear and it has an attractive glossy finish. They represent excellent value for money as a souvenir of Scotland.

Paper posters cost £2.80 inc p&p
Plastic coated cost £3.90 inc p&p

To order these publications, fill in the coupon.

PASTIME PUBLICATIONS

To complement your visit to Scotland, Pastime have produced a series of guides:
Scotland, Home of Golf including details of over 400 courses and clubs; **Scotland for Fishing** with full details of permits, fishing clubs, boat and tackle hire and much more; **Scotland for the Motorist**; places of interest, theatres, galleries, historic buildings, gardens and wildlife reserves; **Scotland for Activity Holidays**.
All are available through Tourist Information Centres and good bookshops, priced £3.95 (£4.50 incl. p&p).

ALL PRICES INCLUDE POSTAGE & PACKAGE

ORDER FORM ON OPPOSITE PAGE

PUBLICATIONS ORDER FORM

Please mark the publications you would like, cut out this section and send it with your cheque, postal order (made payable to the Scottish Tourist Board) or credit card details to:

Holiday Scotland, FREEPOST, Glasgow G3 7BR

Scotland: Hotels and Guest Houses	**£8.50** ☐
Scotland: Bed and Breakfast	**£5.90** ☐
Scotland: Self Catering Accommodation	**£6.20** ☐
Scotland: Camping and Caravan Parks	**£4.40** ☐
Enjoy Scotland Pack	**£8.40** ☐
Touring Map of Scotland	**£3.60** ☐
Touring Guide to Scotland	**£4.80** ☐
Pastime Publications	(each) **£4.50** ☐

POSTERS	Plastic Coated £3.90	Paper £2.80
Piper (24" x 34")	☐	☐
Edinburgh Castle (24" x 34")	☐	☐
Land o' Burns (27" x 40")	☐	☐
Isle of Skye (27" x 40")	☐	☐
Highland Cattle (24" x 34")	☐	☐
Curling (24" x 34")	☐	☐
Scottish Post Boxes (24" x 34")	☐	☐
Five Sisters of Kintail (27" x 40")	☐	☐
Loch Eilt (24" x 34")	☐	☐

BLOCK CAPITALS PLEASE:

NAME (Mr/Mrs/Ms) _____

ADDRESS _____

_____

POST CODE _____ TELEPHONE NO. _____

SIGNATURE _____ DATE _____

TOTAL REMITTANCE ENCLOSED £ _____

PLEASE CHARGE MY *VISA/ACCESS ACCOUNT (*delete as appropriate)

Card No.	☐☐☐☐☐☐☐☐☐☐☐☐☐☐☐☐	Expiry Date ☐☐☐☐

To order BY PHONE: 0345 511 511 (local call rate charged) quoting the items you require and your credit card details. For FREE BROCHURES phone the above number or mark the brochures you would like.

☐ Spring Breaks　　☐ Walking　　☐ Cycling　　☐ Riding/Trekking　　☐ Watersports